IBEX SHOOTING ON THE HIMALAYAS

IBEX SHOOTING ON THE HIMALAYAS

MAJOR NEVILLE TAYLOR

GYAN

Published by

GYAN

Gyan Publishing House
5, Ansari Road
Daryaganj, New Delhi-110002
Phone: 011-47034999, 9811692060
E-mail: books@gyanbooks.com

Distribution Network
gyanbooks.com
India, USA, Canada, UK, Australia

ISBN: 978-93-7225-367-2 (PB)

First Published, 1903

2nd Impression 2025

Printed at: Gyan Press, Delhi.

IBEX SHOOTING ON THE HIMALAYAS
Author: MAJOR NEVILLE TAYLOR

CHYBRA. BEARER. THE BAG, 1895. AUTHOR. LASSOO.

IBEX SHOOTING

ON THE

HIMALAYAS

BY

MAJOR NEVILLE TAYLOR

WITH ILLUSTRATIONS

LONDON

SAMPSON LOW, MARSTON & COMPANY, LTD.

ST. DUNSTAN'S HOUSE, FETTER LANE, E.C.

1903

TO MY GODFATHER

FIELD-MARSHAL

SIR NEVILLE CHAMBERLAIN,

G.C.B., G.C.S.I.

PREFACE

ALTHOUGH I had served in India for ten years in a native regiment, many of the officers of which had had experience of hill shooting, and some of them of ibex shooting in Cashmere, I had found it impossible to gather any idea of the general principles on which an ibex expedition should be conducted, and this partly because sportsmen are as a rule better narrators of incidents than exponents of theories, and partly because they seem to be incapable of grasping the extent of the questioner's ignorance of the conditions which determine the nature of the sport in question; moreover, the training of a young soldier makes him diffident about monopolizing the time of his seniors.

My experience in this matter is a common

one, hence it frequently occurs that the inexperienced find themselves on the wild snowfields of Cashmere in a state of ignorance, which puts them at the mercy of the shikari. They are forced to follow his advice blindly, and chafe unreasonably at the constant halts and wearisome checks which, if their *raison d'être* be not understood, are most exasperating to the keen; they are inexpressibly trying, even if one is lucky enough to have a good and reliable shikari, but reduce the man to despair who has reason to doubt his guide's ability or good faith.

In this case the way is far from smooth. The shikari presumes at first on his master's ignorance, and after a bit the master, who has lost confidence without gaining knowledge, issues orders and interferes generally, in a manner which is fatal to success.

It is undeniable that the necessary information may be quickly acquired on the spot by a man who is familiar with the metaphorical speech of the oriental, and can converse fluently in Hindustani. I lay stress on the word "fluently," for though all shikaris speak Hindustani it is not their mother tongue, and they use it but clumsily. A mere smattering of the lingo, therefore, is not always sufficient to enable the hearer to grasp the full significance of their words.

Hampered as the young sportsman generally is by comparative ignorance both of the native and of his speech, a general knowledge of the habits of the ibex and of the principles on which he is pursued are absolutely essential to the success of the expedition.

This, moreover, in great measure depends on the morale of the whole shooting staff, and on their loyalty and keenness. Knowledge of the points to which shikaris and their assistants attach importance is vital. These men are right good fellows and keen sportsmen, but their health is their capital, and they will not risk it for an egotist who forgets that they are human, with bodies and feelings like his own.

It is with the idea of suggesting these first principles, and of preparing the *debutant* for the chivalrous, manly, but child-like character of his assistants that I have ventured to record my first experiences.

I have not dealt with such matters as maps, routes, arms, and the like, as information on such points becomes rapidly antiquated and is best obtained at the time. I will only remark that with the exception of the rifle, telescope and ammunition, the necessary equipment is best acquired in Srinagar itself. The best shikaris can only be got by means of a letter of introduction, and it is wisest to leave the choice of ground to them.

The points I wish to emphasize are: first, the absolute necessity for some general knowledge of the habits and mode of life of the ibex; and secondly, of the character of the shikari.

The hill-man is a most charming fellow

if taken properly. He is delightful to work with, keen, devoted to his business, hardy and faithful, but he must be handled judiciously. If a man is not prepared to take his fair share of the necessary hardships, and, above all, to be absolutely just and kind withal, he will probably return from Cashmere to swell the numbers of those who think that ibex shooting is an overrated sport.

I have been unable to obtain pictures of the actual valleys which were the scenes of this expedition. The illustrative photographs I have used represent, however, precisely similar adjacent country, and were taken by the Sikkim Boundary Commission. The right to use them was bought from Messrs. Spooner, 379, Strand, London.

NEVILLE TAYLOR.

CONTENTS

LIST OF ILLUSTRATIONS

IBEX SHOOTING ON THE HIMALAYAS

CHAPTER I

PRELIMINARIES

I HAD been given one year's leave, and had made up my mind to spend five months of it shooting in the Himalayas, and the rest in England.

As the dates between which it fell were the 7th of February, 1895, and the 7th of February, 1896, I determined to go first to Cashmere, and then to England.

The land of the ibex lies to the north of the ranges which bound the Cashmere valley proper on the north; the passes leading into it are usually closed by snow till the middle of April, before which, consequently, ibex are not to be got. February and March, however, are the very best months in the whole year for "Barasingha" or Cashmere stags, and for them I accordingly "went," in order to fill up time till April.

It was a terribly hard winter, a severe frost reigned night and day, and the countryside was several feet under snow, which, even as late as the middle of March, showed no signs of melting. The whole land lay enshrouded in a frosty mist, which completely hid the surrounding hills from view. Now and again only did the sun manage to force his way through, while snowstorms of three days' duration were no unfrequent occurrences.

I was uncommonly lucky, however, and managed to get five stags, of which four were real beauties.

Gradually time wore on; and we began to be nervous as to whether some other fellow might not come up soon for ibex, in which case I might not be able to get the "nullah," or valley, which I wanted.

The "leave season" in India is from the 15th of April to the 15th of October; but generally a few men manage to get away by the 1st of April; consequently we determined that nothing would induce us to remain on the wrong side of the passes after the 31st of March.

My "shikari" (or stalker) pointed out that I must not be disappointed if we did not get much sport for the first month, for, he said, the season was a full two months later than usual on account of the severity of the winter. And he added, that when the pass was crossed there would still be two difficulties to encounter. The first being that the hills would be under snow, and consequently there would be no green grass to tempt the ibex down from the crags, where alone there would be grass of any kind, not very palatable stuff certainly, but still food of sorts, growing in the niches of the rocks, where the cliffs were too steep for the snow to lie; to get at our quarry, therefore, would mean hard climbing. And the second, that as the season got warmer all the snow on the steeper places would avalanche, and come down into the valley below; this stage was as a rule over, he said, before people crossed the pass; but this year he feared we should have the benefit of the whole of it. We must, therefore, not be surprised if we were constantly unable to proceed with our stalk. "It *will* happen, sahib," he said, "and it is just as well that you should know what to expect. After a month or so, all the spare stuff will have come down, and the green grass will have sprung up; then instead of having to climb up to the ibex, they will come down to us; and as the snow will have melted a good deal, we shall then be able to get about the hills without difficulty, and shall have an easy time of it, to make up for the first month, which will be hard and dangerous work, and no mistake; and we must not be silly or foolhardy."

The 31st of March, therefore, saw us in a village a few miles from the foot of the pass we were to cross on the morrow. We spent the day in much talking, there being distinct differences of opinion as to the possibility of getting over. The winter had been a very severe one, as I have already said, and the snow in the Cashmere valley even was three feet deep; while where we were, it was some ten feet everywhere, and twenty to thirty feet in the many drifts. But owing to the intense cold its surface had become so firm that the men from the north of the pass had hardened their hearts, and in spite of danger had crossed into the Cashmere valley to get a few luxuries for their great festival day, the Eed; and here they were now collected at the foot of the pass, trying to make up their minds to go back, and yet not liking to be the first to prove it "open" again; I say "again," because a snowstorm had been raging for the last three days, and, though the weather had cleared, the newly-fallen snow was in the avalanching stage, and the road consequently dangerous.

Eventually, about midday, while the final result of this consultation was still doubtful, a messenger from my shikari's village arrived, breathless and weary, with the news that a telegram had just arrived from Srinagar, giving warning that "another sahib had started for the Wardwan." Now the Wardwan was my district; and the only pass into it the "Mergen," near the foot of which we were encamped. If this "other man" and I got over together, we should have a race of 150 miles or so for the best nullah; while if I and my party crossed first, he could hardly hope to catch us up, and would not attempt it, we presumed; and the worry of a protracted race would be avoided.

This settled the question, and an hour more saw us in motion, our object being to reach the very foot of the pass, some six miles off, before sunset, in order to lighten the next day's work, which we foresaw would be long and tiring.

At five in the evening we arrived at our last bit of shelter; great deodars, with their black leaves and stems standing out in bold relief against the white snow. The valley we had been marching up for the last five miles was dense with them, but now they stopped and ran obliquely up the hill on both sides, leaving us face to face with a steep mountain of snow, its top shrouded in a frosty mist. A keen wind blew like a draught down the valley, sighing, whistling and rattling; the black deodars threw their arms wildly overhead, and seemed to warn us against the attempt to cross the forbidding range in front; while the river, flowing under our feet through its continuous tunnel of snow, kept up an ominous bass accompaniment to the wind's high-pitched treble. Something uncanny and eerie weighted my heart, and those of my hillmen; but the thought of "that fellow" behind spurred our courage; and we determined to get over, come snow, come devil.

In an hour the whole scene had changed: the sky was clear, and the kindly little stars were smiling down upon us from a frosty sky, while the moon seemed to promise her light for the ascent, which she fixed at two a.m.

The wind had fallen, and on all sides fires had sprung up, round which could be seen the swarthy faces of the hillmen, as they cooked their modest meals, cracking many a merry jest, while their honest, weather-beaten faces beamed in the light of the huge fires; and with the joyous prospect of being back in their homes, amongst their wives and children, for the Eed, their Christmas.

Later on the "hookah," or pipe, was passed round, and we had a "sing-song," which sounded very monotonous to me, as I could detect no difference in any of the tunes; but we had some grand choruses (if volume be anything), delivered from the brawny chests of some thirty hillmen. The evening broke up with much laughter at a Hindustani song to which I treated them, with topical verses to suit the occasion.

We then repaired to our several fires, which were many, and on a most generous scale, for wood there was in plenty; none of your English fires with split logs, cut up into lengths, but regular bonfires, with the trunk of a fallen tree for a back, and whole trees dragged up, branches and all, their butts crossing one another over a heap of red embers. Presently the trees forming the "back" of the blaze caught fire and glowed with a red heat, brightening to almost white, as the night breeze fanned the crackling embers. Such was the sight that I remember, as, wrapped up in my blankets I lay down to sleep, with my feet towards my own special fire, stretched on a luxurious couch of fine fir branches, which, broken off the trees, formed a green but perfectly dry layer between me and the snow below.

At two a.m. my "bearer," or body servant,

awoke me to a couple of boiled eggs, thick bread and butter, a blue iron teapot, a blue iron teacup with white enamel lining, and an iron milk-jug to match.

It was a lovely night, cold and frosty, with a young moon, and a light night breeze; five minutes later the plate and teapot were empty, my faithful briar was alight, and I was into my second pair of knickerbockers (I had slept in my clothes) and a thick cardigan waistcoat, for there is always a bitter, icy wind on the top of a pass. Everyone else was ready, and within a quarter of an hour of being called we were all in full swing up the hill.

For some three hours we plodded steadily up the hard snow, now and then having to cut ourselves footholds in the steeper places.

Presently the light of the coming day dawned faintly as the moon sank behind the hills; the wind, growing sharper as we neared the top of the pass, seemed fairly to cut through our clothes, while a fine scud blew in our faces from off the crisp surface of the snow, and we suffered many a twinge from the icicles which by now weighed down our moustaches. Half an hour later we were on the top of the pass, and the day had declared itself. In front of us lay the flat plain crowning the pass, from which it takes its name of "Mergen," or plain. One mile more and we had crossed it, and there remained nothing to do but to drop into the valley below.

My shikari, who was in front of me, stopped on the brow of the descent, and I shall never forget the keen animation of his face, as, with an expression something between that of a thoroughbred horse just starting for a race, and of a bloodhound let loose on a track, pointing to the sea of mountain crests towering before us, he exclaimed, "The kingdom of the ibex!"

Even had my legs not so urgently demanded a rest, I should still have stopped involuntarily to survey the land that now lay before me.

It was seven a.m. on a cold, frosty winter's

morning, we were on the top of a pass covered with perhaps twenty feet of snow; on either side, high peaks also deep in virgin snow; in front, two ridges running down and away between them, walled in by their stupendous sides, the narrow valley through which lay our path; and beyond this the mountains proper. What we had come over was, it is true, some 13,000 feet high, but it was a mole-hill compared to the masses we saw in front, rising tier after tier, one behind the other, with their craggy toppling heads virgin white, with great black shadows, silhouetted against the cold glow of the now rising winter's sun.

As I looked towards our road, I saw and grasped what these men, born and bred in the hills, had been afraid of, and I understood it better and better as we steeply climbed down into what seemed a grave. The bottom of the valley we were about to traverse was but some twenty yards wide, and on both sides the snow-clad hills rose to heaven. There was no good objecting now, but it was evident that the risk being run was great; no one spoke, all our eyes were fastened on the white masses of the overhanging hill-side as we plodded through the softening snow, which hung about our feet like clogs, and precluded all idea of haste, even should haste be necessary to life. Occasionally the whole column would stop simultaneously and turn towards a distant spot where an ominous growl and track of smoke marked the long course of an avalanche somewhere up one of the adjacent valleys. The huge masses of snow on both sides of us looked as if they might at any moment slip and engulf us all, and no hope of escape.

It was the 1st of April, and the words "April fool! April fool!" kept ringing in my ears, as I remembered how the pluck of ignorance had made me laugh yesterday at the fears of my far wiser hillmen.

However, the worst part of the road was traversed in an hour or so, and we emerged into a wider, and consequently less dangerous, part of the valley, where we could rest a while, and breathe again without fear of avalanches.

Avalanches! why my idea of an avalanche had been a certain amount of soft snow rumbling down a hill in a cloud of snow-dust; not what I had just seen, namely, the *whole side* of a hill suddenly coming away with a roar like thunder, at the pace of an express train, the mass tearing away everything that came in its way. What were rocks and trees to a thing like that? Just dust before the broom! This huge, irresistible mass would come down perhaps 3,000 feet and foam into the lowest valley, leaving there a huge heap of *débris* a quarter of a mile long, and filling up the valley to a height of perhaps forty feet; a heap of snow, rocks, trees, huge blocks of frozen snow, and snowballs as big as a small house; the wind of the avalanche meantime would set off perhaps twenty more on a smaller scale on both sides of its course.

After an hour's rest, and breakfast, we continued on a similar course, but through a wider and safer valley; but it was laborious work, for the snow was getting softer and softer under the influence of a fierce sun; and we were sinking in well above our knees at every step.

At about noon we had another halt for food and a smoke; and while resting we surveyed the hill opposite through the telescope and glasses, and saw, about two miles off, what we made out to be a very fine ibex, which we determined to leave till next day, and we pursued our way. The character of the country gradually altered as we got lower; the hill-sides were first scattered with a few odd trees, looking lonely and neglected as they stood in sheltered nooks among the snow; then they were dotted here and there with clumps of leafless birch and dark deodars; and, finally, striped with long patches of trees, lying like shadows in the shelter of some cliff, or crowning some less exposed ridge. The day had now warmed up a good deal, and the sun had got a fair view into our valley, so that though I had long since divested myself of my second pair of knickers and my cardigan, and had donned my blue glare-spectacles (as had also the coolies), I was fairly dripping with the exertion and warmth, and was beginning to ask pretty frequently "How much further?" "One *kos* more" was the invariable answer, which put me in mind of the "mile and a bittock," so familiar to those who know bonnie Scotland, and which means anything between one and ten miles.

However, we did at length emerge from our side-valley into the main one, and saw the village of Wardwan on the far side of a small hill river, which we waded. Phew! how cold the water was! and how we held our breath as it came up above our ankles, knees, and finally reached our belts; water which an hour ago had been snow, and which apparently had to keep constantly on the jump to prevent itself from becoming ice.

Ten minutes later, however, we were in a hut, with a roaring fire and a pleasant feeling that now our troubles were over, and our fun about to begin. Then prayers were offered that snow might prevent, and avalanches engulf all who should come after us, until such time as we had got the big chap we had seen on our way.

An hour later we saw our coolies arriving, singing as they crossed the stream in threes and fours, with linked arms, for fear of being washed away; and soon they were with us. Honest fellows! with little clothes and stout legs, they had carried forty pounds each over a pass 13,000 feet high, and along some twenty miles of deep snow, which, fit though I was, had fairly tired me; and here they were, wanting only a word of praise, and two days' wages, to render them as jolly as sandboys. All volunteered to let me know when the "other sahib" should arrive at the pass; and this apparently was not all talk, for my shikari was quite satisfied to wait, and try for my big ibex, until they should bring him news of "that other fellow's" arrival. Then I should be away with the wings of the wind, causing an aching heart and despairing to my rival, who had doubtless hoped to surprise me, and start the race for the best nullah on even terms.

It was now six o'clock in the evening, and, having changed my clothes and had some tea, I had an hour's sleep while my bearer improvised a hasty meal consisting of cocoa, six boiled eggs, bread and butter and honey in the comb, which is good enough, if it does not form the *menu* for more than six days a week. Then a smoke with the shikari, and hey for my "downy," which consisted of blankets, spread on the floor, a couch as good as a feather-bed to a man who does not remember lying down.

IBEX.

CHAPTER II

MY FIRST IBEX

A CLEAR idea of the ibex and his ways is necessary to the proper understanding of my account of my first day after ibex.

The ibex is a goat, standing about as high as a donkey, and very massively built, with horns which sweep up and back in one regular graceful curve. A good horn should be over 35 inches long, and 10 to 11 inches in circumference at the base. He lives to a great age, sometimes it is said reaching fifty years. The beasts themselves vary a good deal in colour; the biggest are generally piebald, that is, have a black head and neck, a beard ten inches long, black at the base and whitish at the ends, a light yellowish body, with black stomach and legs, and a black stripe down the back. They are very shy, and live as high up in the snow as they can; generally coming down at about three in the afternoon to graze below the snow level. Here they spend the night, and having had another good meal in the early morning, they retire at about nine o'clock to some beetling crag, whence they have a perfect view of the steep slopes below, and from whence they again descend at about three in the afternoon, having spent the day in sleep, and in a careful survey of the ground they intend to graze on. They depend chiefly on their eyesight for safety, but have also a very keen sense of smell, and it must not be imagined that they are deaf. They have one weak point, however, they do not anticipate danger from above. Having spent the whole day on the highest point necessary to safety, they seem to dismiss the thought of danger from above: this is the sportsman's greatest hope. Their activity is something wonderful; they will gallop over places a man cannot cross at all; so that when you get a good head, you may be justly proud of your trophy. The ibex generally live in herds of ten or twenty, but old males often live alone, or with only one female, but occasionally herds of thirty are seen. The females are a light yellow colour all over, looking very like sheep, and have short straight horns; they are quicker and cleverer than the ordinary male, though I think a really old male is the cutest of all.

Our party consisted of myself, the head shikari, a second shikari, and a coolie to carry a blanket for each, and a little food; the former in case of long waits in the snow, and the latter for our lunch. We all wore the same kit, namely, a "karki" puggree, Norfolk jacket, flannel shirt, no waistcoat, very loose knickerbockers, putties, cloth socks made with two divisions for the toes, one big one to contain four toes and a smaller one for the big toe. This form of sock is a *sine quâ non*, because "grass shoes" are worn. The grass shoe is simply a pad, about the size of the sole of the foot, plaited out of straw rope, of about the size of an ordinary pencil, with a long loop at the toe, and a sort of rope railing, as it were, running all round it; and besides this there is a long grass rope, with which the shoe is bound on to the foot. To adjust the shoe, you place your foot on the pad, and turn the toe loop up between your big toe and the others, in fact, through the slit in your sock. The long rope is then passed from the toe on one side, through the loop, round the railing, and then back through the toe loop and railing on the other side; across and across the instep about five times, getting nearer the ankle each time, and finishing up with two turns round it, while the railing running round behind the heel prevents the foot from sliding off behind. When put on, you find yourself with a soft pad of matting under your foot, perhaps half an inch thick, and with all your toes over the end of the shoe, and ready to grip with; in them you can keep your footing on anything, as the rough grass plait gets a wonderful grip of stones, snow, rocks, dry grass, and what not. In boots you have no chance except with spikes; and these are very bad on rocky ground, and make a noise, while with grass shoes you can move quite silently. A grass shoe lasts generally one day, but often not half if the ground is stony.

The other essential to hill climbing is what may be called the climber's third leg, namely, the "stick." It is some six feet in length, of a tough hill ash, straight and tapering, from one and a half inch in dia meter at the handle to three-quarters of an inch at the point, which is protected by an iron ferrule, hammered out at the end to a flat head about two inches long and one and a half inch in width, which comes in useful when, as constantly occurs, a foot-hold must be cut in the ice, or in steep grass slopes, whenever, in short, it is not necessary to cut deeper steps with the small hatchet which is also invariably taken.

Imagine us, therefore, about to start for the day. First goes Lassoo, a veteran of forty-five years, who has been at the game since he was a boy of fifteen. A tall spare man is he, broad-chested and strong-limbed, looked up to by all for his honesty, and obeyed implicitly by all as a past master of his craft: see him armed with his faithful stick (which has seen the death of many a veteran ibex, to judge by the marks on its haft), with a small pair of binoculars for the actual stalk, and his telescope, in the use of which he is extraordinarily proficient.

Next comes "Master," with nothing to inconvenience him, as he cannot afford to do anything which would render his unaccustomed feet less sure in the bad places. After him, close behind, follows "Muksooda," the second shikari, a son of old Lassoo; a strong, active man of twenty-five, who is learning his work, and carries the rifle; and also, though this you are not told, sticks closely to you in case of a slip, and many a time had I to thank him for that

THE START.

firm touch which seemed just to decide whether I went down a few thousand feet or not. Lastly, with beaming and somewhat stupid countenance, follows the "lunch coolie," as he is called, one Chybra by name. A real man of the mountains is he, and as at home among them as the ibex himself; and well he needs be, for he has to follow as best he can with three blankets and our lunch, together with three or four pairs of grass shoes, slung over his shoulders in a blanket, which crossing over his chest and tied behind his back leaves his hands free: the hatchet stuck in his belt completes his picture.

Four men from the village came as far as yesterday's stream, over which they carried us; and then we continued up yesterday's valley.

After proceeding at leisure some four miles, we were stopped by Lassoo, who went on to reconnoitre; we followed some two hundred yards behind, advancing when he did, and stopping when he sat down to search with the telescope each valley as it opened up to the right. See with what infinite pains he scans each valley, sitting in the least exposed place he can find, with his stick stuck firmly into the snow before him, while his left hand grasps the stick and the far end of the telescope, and his right holds the eye-piece of the glass steady to the eye, thanks to the support of his right knee and elbow. Nothing in that valley. On he goes, taking advantage of all cover, and never exposing himself; then a careful search of the next one; and on again. We had been advancing in this way for perhaps a mile, Lassoo was sitting in his usual position, and we were beginning to get a bit doubtful, when suddenly he brought down the glass, crawled to the side of our valley, and sitting down under the cover of an overhanging rock, beckoned to us to come to him carefully. On our arrival, and in answer to my question, "What's up?" he replied, "I've seen him," while his face shone with anticipation and relief.

But apparently the ibex were on the move, and we could not go on for a bit. Five minutes later Lassoo crawled forth again for another look, and saw them still going up and up, and still commanding our valley at a point where it was met by theirs; but approaching a spot whence, for a minute only, they would not be able to do so. "Get ready, now!" came the order, and we all got up, and waited. "Now, come on!" was the word, and we all went across the hundred yards of valley as fast as bent bodies and the soft snow permitted. From there Lassoo again reconnoitred, and presently came back with a beaming face to say that the ibex had taken up their position on that very rock behind which they had just gone. We had got across in the very nick of time, for no one could cross in front of their valley now without being seen; and there was no possible route up the hill on the village side. The first part of our stalk would now be simple, for we had now only to climb up the next valley, having a ridge between us and the ibex the whole way; once level with them we should have to wait until they moved in the evening, and then be guided by circumstances.

A steep climb of some three hours, up a slope of short dry grass, brought us to the level of our friends. Here we were aided by a narrow streak of deodars which crowned the top of the intervening ridge, and from their friendly shelter we could at leisure survey the much-coveted prize, the patriarch of the herd, as he lay on his hard bed of solid rock, gazing down into the valley beneath, shifting his position now and again, generally lying as a cow does, with his head raised and chewing the cud, while his long beard floated out on the mountain breeze; sometimes stretching himself out at full length on his side with his head pillowed on a rock, and anon brushing the flies off his back with a sudden sweep of his horns, or indulging in an ecstatic scratch at the root of his tail with first one horn and then the other. At times he would get up and walk sleepily a few yards, then lie down again, like a dog, with his head between his forefeet, and his horns lying on either side of his back. Little thought had he of danger, for were not his two wives with him, and had they ever failed to warn him during the last fifty years! and well they justified his confidence, for during the six hours we lay there waiting in the snow never once did they relax their vigilance, but with heads on one side carefully searched the ground below them.

We meanwhile (having arrived at about ten) set up the telescope at them, and then lay down, wrapped in our rugs and ate, slept, and tried to keep warm on our snow bed, while one man was kept constantly at the glass to give warning if the animals showed any signs of changing their position, for all my men knew that our quarry would not make a big move till three or four in the afternoon. However, to me it was different, for I had never even seen an ibex before, and I lay for hours with my eye to the telescope watching their every movement. Although they were half a mile away, yet looking through the telescope they seemed quite close, and the notches on the old man's horns were distinctly visible, as was also his beard, and even his eyes; a dozen times my heart stood still as the watchful females seemed to be looking right down the telescope, and we appeared to have been discovered; then with a sigh of relief I dropped my head from the glass, as they looked just as anxiously in the opposite direction. I then essayed to sleep, but my nerves were on the jump, and not to be quieted; so I went off to where Lassoo was lying, calmly smoking his hookah.

"How big do you think his horns are, Lassoo?"

"Nearly forty inches."

"Do you think we shall get him?"

"God only knows."

"What will you do if he grazes this way, because between us will be all open snow?"

"We shall have to go home and try again to-morrow."

"But it may take a week at that rate to get even a shot!"

"Yes; but a week is better than a month."

"Well, any way, the wind is favourable, and blowing from him towards us."

"Yes, just now; but it may change."

"But I'm sure he will graze the other way, and then we shall have his ridge between us, and will only have to get across that bit of snow, and from there there's lots of cover."

Lassoo turned his face towards me and said:

"Sahib, that's just the point: now listen to me. You see that ibex, and you see where we are; there's nothing between us except two hundred yards of open snow and some three hundred yards of broken ground beyond. Once over that snow and we should have a good chance of a shot, *but that snow is going to avalanche*; it may go any minute, and it may not go till to-morrow, but going it is. We shall take about two minutes going across it; do you think it good enough to risk it?"

"How do you know it's going to avalanche?" said Incredulity.

Lassoo merely stroked his beard and said quietly:

"Sahib, when I first came on to these hills I had no beard. But I think that if the snow is still there when we want to go it's worth risking it, as he's a lovely beast," and his eyes glittered hungrily.

"All right, that's settled," said I, thinking him a nervous old fool.

How the time lags! Why it's only one! Then another look through the glass, during which I am apparently discovered three times by each of the females, then back to Lassoo, who still smoked on perfectly placidly.

"How big do you think he is, Lassoo?"

"Nearly forty inches."

"Do you think he will move soon?"

"Not before three."

Another look at my watch, which showed 1.30.

I thought it would never be three.

"You'd better have a sleep, sahib!" says Lassoo.

Sleep! Why, you might just as well ask a bride to sleep at the altar. However, I sat apart, and smoked; looked at my watch; and lay down again; wriggled about; and had another look at it; listened to hear if the watch had stopped; and then had another pipe. However, the longest lane has a turning, and three did come at last, and everyone began to show a little animation; even the imperturbable Lassoo had a look through the glass; but soon came away again, and resumed his seat; while Muksooda took his place at the telescope. Everyone was ready and waiting, when presently the report came, "The big one's up." Lassoo was at the glass in a moment, and kept up a running account of the proceedings. "Male grazing this way —one female gone over the other side of the ridge—that female come back again."

Visions floated before me of going back after all without a shot; for if they grazed towards us, we could not move in their direction without being seen. "Now the females are on the ridge": indeed, you could now see them with the naked eye, as their figures stood out clearly on the sky-line. "Now they're making up their minds which way to go. Allah be praised! they've gone over the other side in earnest, and at a gallop, and the male will follow them to a certainty."

Lassoo rose, the telescope was shut up with a snap and returned to its case, and we all stood ready behind the trees. Then the big one walked lazily on to the crest and had a look round. Lassoo was like a grey-hound on the leash, as with goggling eyes he watched his prey, and, with a warning palm towards us, awaited the moment when the male should disappear and leave our way open. The ibex stood a moment on the ridge, and then went over with a will on the other side.

"Come!" and Lassoo was away at a hard run, we following. "Go as you please" was the order of the day, and we went the best pace we could, over our knees in snow, sometimes plunging in nearly to our armpits, which prevented of course any risk of our losing foothold, steeply though the snow sloped away to our right. A couple of minutes of this, and we were safely across the snow and under cover, and could sit down awhile to get our breath again.

As we crossed this steep snow slope I noticed, as I plunged deep into it, that there was some six inches of hollow between the bottom of the snow and the ground, due of course to the melting of the snow, so that all that was keeping this snow up at all, was the adhesion at the sides; this Lassoo had somehow or other divined, and hence his fears.

"Allah be praised, we are safely over, and now I think we shall get him," said Lassoo, while a handful of fine snow dust thrown up showing the wind to be still from the game, and towards us, proclaimed our chances good. Onward we crept till we reached the place from which Lassoo expected to see them; there we halted and loaded the rifle. Lassoo then crept on, alone, but soon shook his hand to show that he had seen nothing; then, with a blank look on his face threw up a little snow dust; it blew towards the ibex! The wind had changed! or there was a local eddy! I, too, felt that the wind was on the back of my wet neck and not on my face, as before. Lassoo wriggled on like a worm, peered round the corner for a second, and then came quickly back; and as he passed me whispered, "Come along, sahib, as hard as you can, I've seen him; they have winded us, and are going slowly up; we must race up the other side of this ridge, and try to get a shot as they cross." We retraced our steps a bit, and then up we went at something little short of a run. Soon my legs began to feel weak, but I could not stand being beaten by Chybra, who, though carrying a load, was now "leading" me. No one was *thinking* even of a second's rest, and so from pure shame I stuck to it, and we all strained up the steep ascent, the bulk of the work falling to our hands and toes. My breath came short and quick, my heart felt like bursting, and the pulses of my temples sounded like hammers on an anvil; but still they hurried on, until absolutely exhausted I sank on to my face, done! Go further without rest I simply could not. Almost as I collapsed I heard the warning "Hist," and, looking, saw everyone flat on his face, while one of Lassoo's fingers seemed to point straight upwards towards a great buttress of rock sticking boldly out towards us on the ridge. I involuntarily turned my eyes in the direction indicated, and there, sure enough, the points of two horns were visible and moving; the horns becoming more and more apparent, until quite suddenly the whole ibex came to view, two hundred yards off. There he stood, high above us, looking down at us in an incredulous way, only his forelegs, chest and head visible, as with head alternately on one side and the other, he seemed to wonder what these prostrate forms could be, if forms indeed they were, up at this unwonted time of the year in his own special preserves.

I was so out of breath that to fire would have been useless; so with a groan I bowed my head to the ground, and did not move for a full minute. When I looked again he was still there; something must be done soon, or not at all: so I slowly got my rifle into position, took as steady an aim as I could at his chest, which was all I could see, and pressed the trigger. I knew it was a shaky shot, but I could not expect him to stand there for ever. "Bang" went the rifle, but the ibex did not seem to notice it, as he stood for a moment, and then slowly turning round moved up the hill, and out of sight. Almost immediately the two females crossed a small snow valley, which divided their ridge from the next one on my left. If the big one should cross the same way I had yet a chance, and by this time I had got my breath and was quite steady. Half a minute perhaps after this the male emerged, walked slowly across the snow, and, when fairly in the middle, stopped and surveyed us curiously. Now was my chance, and I fired absolutely steady at three hundred yards. He turned round sharply, slipping a little as he did so, and was out of sight. I flung myself on my back, and despair seized my heart, although Lassoo went off to see if he were wounded, which he said he thought he was. I lit my pipe, and gave myself up to the bitterest reflections.

Presently I heard a slight whoop from

above, and was instantly fallen upon by Muksooda, who proceeded to hammer me on the back with his clenched fist, nearly knocking me down the hill, with such violence did he wring my hand in both his, as he shouted, "Well done, sahib, we've got the forty-incher!" The next moment I was attacked in a similar manner by Chybra, if you please, and looking up I saw the figure of a man tobogganning down the slope, sitting astride on the body of the ibex, holding a horn in his left hand, while he waved his right over his head, reeling about like a drunken man singing a drunken song. Could this be my phlegmatic friend of the morning? I could hardly believe it, yet he it was.

After a careful measurement of the horns, one of which proved to be 40 inches, and the other 40½ inches in length, more hand-shaking, and a pipe, we proceeded down the hill, Chybra keeping the body on the slide down the small snow nullah, while we walked down the ridge dividing it from the main one on our right, which we had first crossed. While going I asked Lassoo where he had found the ibex, and he told me that he had found it quite dead, shot through the heart, about fifty yards from where it had been when I fired.

Now that the excitement was over I think that we all felt that peculiar sensation which follows the successful attainment of a much-coveted object. There was a sort of warm glow in my brain, and a feeling of absolute content about my heart; while ever and anon I could not help looking down into the nullah on our left, where the ibex was being ruthlessly shoved along by Chybra in long slides of perhaps a hundred yards at a time; now getting hung up by a horn, the graceful curve of which would now and again catch up in some soft piece of snow, into which it embedded itself like an anchor, and when freed from this, would go sliding on, sometimes turning over and over slowly, as the surface of the snow, rough in places, caught a grip of the hair; at other times going now head foremost, and now tail foremost, but always in that curiously limp and boneless manner characteristic of a dead body before time has stiffened its limbs, and leaving a trail of blood over the white surface of the snow.

Yes, there he was, and no mistake, the fine chap we had so longed to get. And yet a moment later I had to look again to see that there was no mistake about it, and that I had not been dreaming.

And I fell a-thinking how his head would look in the hall of our home in England, and how my people would prize it; of the way it would be pointed out to our friends when they came to stay with us; of the yarns I would spin, believed by some, and pretended to be believed by others; of the way the fellows in the mess would take it, when the letter was read out to them in the sultry plains of India, where they were taking chloroform pegs to get an appetite for breakfast, and how all would be pleased in their various ways. I could imagine

Sammy saying, "Great fun, I should think, if you could only ride it"; George, "What a pity it is such lonely work"; Peter, with eyes twinkling with pleasure, and the remembrance of his own exploits, but saying only, "Really, a forty-incher, what a lucky chap"; and Gobby's, "I'm glad the boy has got a good one"; while Mac would merely look delighted and say nothing. Badger was, I had heard, shooting bison and tiger in Central India—how I hoped he would get a real good head! All the others would be away, but if they . . . C-r-r-r-a-a-ck! C-r-r-r-a-a-ck! came ringing from the big nullah on my right, that peculiar noise which we have all heard when skating, which rings round and round the edge of the lake as the ice disengages itself from the sides. C-r-r-r-a-a-ck! C-r-r-r-a-a-ck! came the echo back, multiplied from the hills. I felt my arm seized by Lassoo, but he said only, "Now look!" and looking, I saw, and stood aghast. The whole of the snow in that valley in front of us seemed to move, just an inch at first, then quicker; and in a second the whole mass was fairly under way — smoothly and almost silently at first, and then, as if tired of such a decorous proceeding, it suddenly broke up with loud, sharp reports, and foaming back from the sides of the narrowing gorge, tore along with a bass deafening roar, in which the voice of the huge rocks, rolling along under the snow, was still audible. On went the river of snow, getting deeper and deeper as its bed grew narrower, and finally fell like Niagara into the valley below, while behind it came the usual following of rocks and stones, which seemed not to have made up their minds to go till too late, and to be hurrying now to catch up; while from all sides came the echoes, giving a jumbled second edition.

I looked at Lassoo, who pointed up to where we had been waiting, watching the ibex the whole day, and with his finger traced where our track across that very valley had been, and which now was not, saying quite quietly, "Sahib, you can trust a hillman with a beard"; while I felt very small as I remembered my thought of the morning, "nervous old fool," though with a friendly pat on his shoulder I said, "It would have been hard lines if it had selected the very two minutes we were crossing it to go and do that."

He understood and accepted the apology, and we went down the hill.

CHAPTER III

AN OFF-DAY

HAVING skinned the ibex, and taken his head complete, we hurried on, getting back about dark to the hut in which my abode had been taken. After a good square meal off very tough mutton I was soon asleep, and lay like a dead man till morning, with the knowledge that four a.m. was to see us off towards our nullah, the Krish; for Lassoo's idea was to get into its vicinity and to make darts up the adjoining valleys before fellows came over.

What was my surprise, therefore, on waking, to find that it was eight o'clock. I shouted to my "bearer," who told me that it had been snowing hard the whole night; that there was no sign of change, and that Lassoo had left a message advising an "easy," as we could not move that day. I accordingly made up my mind to have a "Europe morning," had breakfast in bed, a pipe, and a most delicious snooze, not getting up till ten o'clock; after which, having had another meal, I sallied out to have a look at the head.

Lassoo and the coolies had appropriated an adjoining hut, and in one of its rooms I found them all; Lassoo smoking and looking on, Muksooda and the coolies hard at work. The skin had been pegged out tight on the ground, hair downwards, and the coolies were engaged in removing the bits of flesh that had been left sticking to the hide when the beast was skinned. To Muksooda had been confided the more difficult task of cleaning the head. All superfluous matter having been carefully cut off, the skin was well rubbed with saltpetre, and left to dry. I was then taken into another room to see the horns, which were hanging from a beam. Chybra was made to put them on his head, which he did with great gusto, arching his neck and looking, he imagined, like an ibex.

This took us to lunch time, which meal was followed by an hour's letter writing, and a couple of hours' reading. I had plenty of literature, as I had subscribed to the very excellent Srinagar library. I could have six volumes at a time, which I changed whenever I had occasion to send for letters and supplies. I was lucky enough to have a lady friend in Srinagar who chose my books for me, and I owe her a debt of gratitude for the skill she showed in her selections. These books were, of course, only used for reading indoors; I had sixpenny editions of Dickens, Thackeray, etc., which I took up the hill with me daily, and which, as might be expected, got hopelessly spoilt.

Getting tired of sitting indoors, I thought I would have a stroll outside, especially as it had left off snowing, and the clouds were rolling away.

I emerged, therefore, into the "village,"

as it is called. It consisted of four huts in all, of very much the same pattern, viz., two storeys and an attic. They were built of pine logs in the rough, were wainscoted with split logs, and had a thatched roof. The cattle live on the ground floor, the people on the first, and the fowls in the attic. There were generally two living rooms, one used as a general bedroom for the family, as well as a combination dining-room, drawing-room and kitchen; and the other a store and workroom, usually containing a hand-loom, on which the whole family were engaged at this season of the year, making clothes for their own use; the father and the big boys working the actual loom, while the little chaps from six years old and upwards made the wool into thread, wound the thread into reels for use, and did suchlike detail work.

Its human inhabitants had been cleared out of my hut, which was exclusively reserved for me and my bearer, as Lassoo would not risk my being disturbed by squalling babies, or other similar annoyances.

Each room had a huge fireplace in the corner, with a hole in the ceiling as a chimney, while a sort of false chimney, made by boarding off the corner from the ceiling to within a few feet of the fireplace, tempted the smoke up towards the hole in the ceiling. This chimney opened into the attic, where all the grain was stored, and where the cocks and hens lived, so that a roaring fire could not be permitted for fear of lighting the thatch or the grain.

I was very comfortable in my hut, but there were drawbacks.

One was due to the primitive nature of the windows, which were merely holes, two feet square, with wooden doors, glass being an unattainable luxury in those parts. It was consequently impossible to exclude the cold outer air without producing utter darkness. Should the occupant wish to read, he was forced to open the shutter and sit shivering in the opening, or else in the doorway.

The behaviour of the fowls was another.

They live, poor brutes, in the attic, which they habitually enter, not by the ample space between the eaves and the wall, but by the window of the dwelling-room below and by the chimney.

Their *modus operandi* is the following. I give a typical instance.

A hen will be seized by an insane passion for home, to gratify which, after several false starts, she flutters heavily on to the window-sill, squawking vociferously, and remains there some minutes in the near proximity of the reader, screaming as she tries to make up her mind to pass him and enter the room.

If not dislodged by a missile, she presently flutters in, screeching, and makes for the chimney, up which she struggles clumsily, still screeching and fluttering. Nor does the exasperating clamour cease with her arrival, for she keeps up a self-congratulatory cackle for some minutes afterwards.

Should the human being be unable to endure the ten minutes' doubt on the window-sill, and drive the intruder away, his sufferings will be augmented tenfold, for then my lady will sit below, cackling continuously, and, being persistent, will eventually have another try.

Undoubtedly the best policy is to bow to the inevitable, and get it over as quickly as possible.

I am proud to say I achieved this on one occasion, thereby saving myself ten minutes of impotent rage, besides defrauding the hen of half her pleasure, which is malicious.

The cats and rats, too, are very aggravating. Nothing edible must be left in the room if sleep be desired; leave the remains of after-dinner tea on the table and to a certainty a cat will come in in the middle of the night, and upset the whole show on the floor with a crash.

A short wander round to see how the

ibex was progressing, and a look in at the coolies, who were having a big dinner which I had stood them in honour of my first ibex, brought seven o'clock round, and my dinner also; after which I went over to Lassoo's hut for a pipe and a chat. There I found a big congregation of coolies and shikaris having their evening smoke round the fire. I was escorted to the place of honour on Lassoo's right; and a very comfortable seat it was, on a couple of folded blankets with the wall for a "back." Everybody was in great feather after a real heavy meal; and after I had issued some "Pioneer" tobacco for the hookahs, each and all were in a mood for anything. As we sat and talked the hookah went its round, giving out its friendly bubbling sound as one man after another had his three or four pulls at it, and passed it on; while the fire threw a bright red light through the room, now and again lighting up the faces of the hillmen more distinctly as it blazed up under the compulsion of a stamp from a bare foot, or when a fresh log of resinous pine was thrown upon it.

"Now, sahib," said Lassoo, "tell us about the sea," that never-ending source of wonder to men who have never seen anything bigger than the Jhelum river. "Or," exclaimed Chybra, "about the ships; for a sahib once told me that they were as big as a hundred of our biggest boats, and went like trains." "Harput!" said Lassoo, "who are you that you should talk?" Now "harput" means "bear," and I concluded from the context that to be called a "bear" is not a compliment. "Why," said I, "is a bear as stupid as Chybra?" This raised a titter, and Chybra appeared to curl up, though I thought I saw a dangerous look in his eye. "No," said Lassoo, "not as stupid as Chybra—how could he be? but he is the biggest fool in the jungle. I once saw one chase a herd of ibex into some crags which were too steep for him; so he stood at the bottom and roared, in the hope that they would fall down from fright; the ibex meanwhile lay down and went to sleep in perfect security, knowing how safe they were."

"And I," said a coolie, "once saw a bear having a fight with a leopard in a wood. The leopard got behind a tree and showed his face round the corner: the bear had a smack at him, which the leopard easily eluded by withdrawing his head, and the bear hurt his hand against the tree; this one trick he played again and again for some five minutes, until the bear had reduced his hands to pulp; he was examining his injuries when the leopard suddenly taking him unawares, caught him by the throat and killed him."

"That's true," said Lassoo. "If you want to learn stalking, watch a leopard; he is the shikari's tutor."

"Now, I'll tell you a story," said Muksooda, "which I'll swear to on the Koran, as I saw it with my own eyes. I was out with a party from our village after musk deer, about eight years ago, before the order was issued forbidding us to shoot them. We were sitting, having an 'easy' in the middle of the day, when our attention was attracted by a red bear on the hill opposite. He was behaving in the most extraordinary way; now creeping up to the edge of the cliff and looking over, then running back a few yards and sitting down; then coming gingerly to the edge again, and again withdrawing. Presently he seemed to get an idea: after searching about he picked up a big stone in his arms, and approaching the edge deposited it with great care, and again creeping up to the edge looked over very carefully. Yet again he withdrew, picked up the rock in his arms, and deliberately dropped it over the cliff, then took to his heels, running about two miles without stopping. After about an hour he returned, again looked for some time over the edge of the cliff, and then went away leisurely. Impelled by curiosity we went over to see if we could get any clue to this extraordinary behaviour. In time we arrived at the place where the bear had been, and on looking over, as he had done, saw to our surprise a leopard's body lying on a ledge twenty feet below, with his head smashed to atoms by the stone the bear had dropped on to him. The leopard had evidently been asleep there, and the bear coming across him accidentally, saw his chance, but was very afraid of being caught in the act. So having eventually made up his mind, and having dropped the rock, he fled for fear of having missed; but when no signs of the avenging leopard were seen returned to make sure of his success; and then went away satisfied."

I looked incredulously towards Lassoo; but he answered my look with, "That story is true enough, sahib, for has not Muksooda sworn to it on the Koran, and, besides, he told me about it at the time, and his account was corroborated by five or six others who were out with him. You know bears constantly break open the trunks of trees with stones, when they are after honey, and cannot manage it with their claws alone. I've seen them several times doing it: they take the stone in their arms, and dash it against the place they want to break in, doing it again and again, until they have attained their object."

"And I," broke in Chybra, "saw one once who had done that and failed, so what does the harput do? He pulls up green saplings and twists them into a withy, and ties them round his waist like a belt; then he picks up a rock as big as a boy, jambs it in between the withy and his body, and having thus got his hands free, he climbs up the tree, pulls out his rock, and batters the trunk in easily. The harput isn't such a fool as he looks!"

The coolies nearest Chybra proceeded to fall on him, hand and tongue, for a liar; while in an interval in the general laughter, in which Lassoo freely joined, I remarked, "I don't think the harput is such a fool, eh Lassoo? for he had you fairly that time."

The evening broke up after this; everybody went off in high good humour, all except Chybra, who looked very "cheap," so thinking to cheer him up, I said, "I think you won this evening, Chybra." But he, seeing that Lassoo had heard, put on his most shamefaced look, which consisted in seizing both his ears with both his hands at once, at the same time putting his tongue out, catching it between his teeth, and saying, "*hey toba, hai hai hai*" (which being translated means "never could I do such a thing! alas! alas! alas!") "for is not he the greatest of shikaris, while I am only a poor coolie who lives in his shadow?" But all the same his eyes twinkled when Lassoo's back was turned.

It was about ten o'clock when I got into bed, and I was soon fast asleep.

Probably about midnight I was gradually awakened by sounds of something moving in the room; now a board creaked, and now a spoon fell to the ground. I was sleepy and determined not to wake; but gradually it was borne in upon me that the attempt was useless, and I had better get rid of the nuisance; so I hissed out "hish" at the top of my voice, at the same time waving my hands in the dark, and skinning my knuckles against the wall. The noise ceased. I sucked my knuckles, and in five minutes was dropping off to sleep when that vile noise began again. This time I determined I would not awake, so I kept my eyes tightly shut, and held on. However, the fates were against me; a knife clattered to the ground, and a teapot following suit awoke me in a fury. A moment's careful listening and I had located my enemy, and flung a boot hard at him. There was a crash, over went the table and everything on it, and a scrambling of claws showed that my enemy, a hungry cat evidently, had escaped by the chimney. After this I thought I had better see the whole thing out; so I lighted a candle and had a look. Such a mess as there was! The table had been knocked over; the floor was littered with rice and chicken bones (the remains of my last night's curry); the teapot had emptied cold tea and tea-leaves over my knickers for to-morrow, and my shirt was soaked with the best unadulterated milk; so I thought I would go and awaken my "bearer," just as a lesson not to leave my dinner things in the room at night; a thing I'd warned him against a dozen times. I therefore went, candle in hand, towards the veranda, but the moment the door opened my candle was blown out by a gust of wind. I could not find the matches; and as I was getting beastly cold I went to get a light from the embers of the fire; *en route*, of course, I trod into the cold milk on the floor, and jumping out of that, landed on the prongs of the fork, and ran a splinter of wood into my other foot. However, my candle and I did eventually reach the fire; but to-night candle-grease was apparently not inflammable, and I could not raise a flame to save my life! So I yelled for the bearer; row enough to awaken the dead. I then listened. Not a sound! Then I thought I would go to bed; but if I did I knew that brute of a cat would come back again and wake me up. So I determined to find the matches, as they must be somewhere near the bed. I reached the bed all right, after having trod on my iron teapot and hit my head against a coat-peg in the wall; but no matches could be found. I bethought me of the small case I always carried in my clothes; I felt in my coat under my pillow, and threw that away in disgust; in all my waistcoat pockets, never a sign! grovelled about on the floor to see if my treasure had fallen, but no result; and I should have been looking till morning if I hadn't accidentally put my hand into the pocket of the knickers I was wearing, and there was the box! Then I re-lighted the candle and went towards the bearer's room, next door to mine, mind you, with between us only a wooden partition which did not come within three feet of the ceiling. Just what I expected! There he was, with his head underneath the blankets, sound asleep, and I firmly believe that the last trumpet wouldn't have awakened him before his proper rising hour of four a.m. However, a shake did; and I led him, half asleep, into my room, which he surveyed in horror. And a sight it was! A stream of milk half way across the floor; cups, saucers, teapot, tea-leaves, knives, forks, spoons, books, clothes, rice, and chicken bones scattered about, while I stood in the midst of the *débris* in a flannel-shirt and knickers (my night garments on the expedition) with the candle high over my head, and wrath in my bleary eyes, pointing at the mess! I think he thought I had gone mad, but I soon explained the position, and left him to make a blaze and straighten things up a bit, while I had a smoke by the fire. That was the last time he left my dinner things in my room at night. By the time the pipe was smoked out the room was tidy again, the milk and tea wiped up, my wet clothes hung up by the fire to dry, and everything edible removed, while the cat's return by the chimney was provided against by a roaring fire. Thus ended my adventures for the night, and I slept undisturbed till called at four a.m.

CHAPTER IV

KRISH NULLAH

A COUPLE of days double-marching brought us to the foot of our nullah, the Krish, and we had reached the place called "Gurm Pani," or hot springs, a recognized point, the attainment of which gave us the sole right of shooting the Krish; so now we had no further cares on that score.

It was a quaint sort of spot this "Gurm Pani." The river of snow water, surging along through the valley, was bounded on one side by steep hills, running down to the river, covered with birch and fir forests, the birch of course quite bare, with silver stems, and the firs very black amidst their snow surroundings. The other side consisted of absolutely precipitous cliffs, with a narrow plain, some one hundred yards in width, between the cliffs and the river. On this plain our tents were pitched for the first time during the expedition, and this gave us the pleasant feeling that now business was about to begin in real earnest.

The hot springs were close down by the river itself, and only a few feet above the flood. They are of some repute, and people with rheumatism are in the habit of bathing in them when the weather is warmer. For their convenience the Cashmere government had built a very comfortable wooden shed, with a boarded floor, and open on all sides, with the exception of a three-foot boarding along the two long sides as a protection from the wind. Over the spring itself a rough wooden roof has been constructed. I had a bathe myself, and enjoyed it very much, as I had not had a bath for a month. The water inside the bathing-shed was about two feet deep, and just comfortably hot; bubbling up at one end, and running out into the river at the other, with a bottom of fine white pebbles; a most luxurious bath of some five yards square. One had to be careful of oneself for awhile afterwards; for after a regular Turkish bath it was rather a sudden change to come out into an air which was "fresh" to say the least of it, with a snow-water river running only a few feet off. Just now there were no people there; but when I came back that way, three months afterwards, there were a great number. By the shed were various fires, over which parties were sitting making tea; beside them stood big piles of "chupatties," or unleavened cakes, which seemed to be part of the cure. The course of treatment is as follows:—First the patient has a Turkish bath, after which he wraps himself up in a vast number of shawls and blankets, lies down in the shed and perspires, aided by hot tea and "chupatties." As soon as he has cooled down a bit, he has another bath, more blankets and tea and so on, *ad lib.*, continuing the process for as many days or weeks as he thinks fit. Now, however, we had the whole place to ourselves.

Several friends of Lassoo came in at intervals during the day to greet him and to bring information about the adjoining nullahs. These reports were far from satisfactory, so we decided to abstain from harrying the nullahs, and to confine ourselves to our own proper hunting-grounds.

Next day, therefore, we continued our course for some five or six miles to the village of Metwan, which was the last village we should see. On arrival we had a careful survey of the hills, and to our joy spotted a herd, with one very fine head in it. We made up our minds to stay there till we should get it, for there was no occasion to hurry, as the valley further up was still too deep in snow to be accessible in the shooting sense.

The afternoon was spent in watching the herd as they left their day's outlook post and came down the hill to their grazing-ground. As they generally spend the night near where they happen to be at nightfall, it was very important to exactly locate the place where we might expect to find them next morning. Consequently, at about three o'clock in the afternoon we turned out with glasses to watch them. There they were, still on their post, mostly asleep, with one or two females already up, and picking the odd bits of dry grass which grew in the cracks on the face of the cliff, but still the patriarch sat on his pinnacle. Then an impatient female galloped coquettishly down a few yards, and looked inquiringly back for permission; but no, his lordship made never a move; then the smaller males got up and looked about; finally, the master of the herd rose with dignity, stretching his stiff limbs and yawning; then all but he came waltzing down the mountain side as if it had been a ball-room floor instead of an almost inaccessible crag. The chief meanwhile surveyed them from above till they had come down perhaps three hundred yards, when suddenly down he came, like a falling rock, and I caught my breath as I held him at the end of the telescope, for he looked as if he must fall, and be dashed to bits; but no, a minute later and he was with the herd grazing placidly. They had by this time reached the higher patches of grass, and extended in groups of three and four (we counted twenty in all) and grazed about, coming slowly downwards, while the sun sank behind the range. As he withdrew his fierce rays, the air began to strike cold; for cold as it was, the sun was very powerful and we were often glad enough to get into the friendly shade of a rock or tree; not for long though, for we soon felt the cold again, and were glad of his warming beams once more.

Gradually the herd seemed to point in one direction, and finally, as it was getting dark, one of the younger males took up his post on one of the lower buttress-like rocks, and all gradually grouped themselves round him for the night.

It was now too dark to see, so we went back to the camp fire, and warmed ourselves till dinner. After dinner Lassoo came over to my hut for his usual after-dinner chat, a thing I always looked forward to, for Lassoo was a man of brains, and could understand anything; and such a nature's gentleman that it was always a pleasure to talk with him. I know no one who was a better listener, and few with such a variety of experiences; I learned more about how to manage a Cashmeri in five months' talk with him, than I could have done in two years if I had only my own experience to guide me.

Then we made our plans for the morrow. Lassoo said that we could easily get near the ibex if they stayed where they were; but that if they moved much, the ground would be awkward, and that consequently we must get up level with them, by dawn if possible. There would be a good moon at three, he said, and the route along a well-defined valley running right up the hill was very fairly easy; so that if we were on foot at three, we might expect to be near them at seven, as they were comparatively low down. When Lassoo had gone, and my lunch had been packed in readiness for an early start, and orders given for bread and butter, boiled eggs and tea for 2.30 a.m., we all turned in, so as to be "fit" to-morrow. At 2.30 breakfast was produced, and then Muksooda came in as usual to put on my grass shoes and putties; and three o'clock saw us fairly on foot.

A bitterly cold morning it was, with a piercing wind, and a bright moon, but rather cloudy. We walked fast at first to keep warm; but after ten minutes' climbing our foreheads were studded with beads of perspiration, while our moustaches began to hang with icicles. On and on we went, till, after an hour and a half's stiff climbing, Lassoo called a halt, for we had got to rather an awkward place, and it was just as well to wait a quarter of an hour until the now dawning light should grow a little stronger. Then on again we went, the stars getting paler in the sky as the day gradually declared itself, until 6.30 saw us up at the very top of the valley we had been ascending. Then a five minutes' rest, while Lassoo preceded us some yards to reconnoitre, coming back immediately to say that the ibex were level with us, about eight hundred yards off. A short stalk brought us within two hundred yards of them, with only one open valley between us, so that evidently we could hope to get no nearer. We could not make out, for certain, which was the biggest of the three males we saw. Lassoo got his telescope out, and after a careful look at them, pronounced our quarry to be the light-coloured piebald whom we could just see near a rock in the snow; and handed me the glass so that I could make certain. I was about to look, when suddenly the whole herd went off at a slow canter, round the corner of the hill, and out of sight. I was for following them up, but Lassoo said it was not the right thing to do. "No," he said, "we will get under cover till the afternoon, and then have another try, because they are not really frightened, and will be quite pacified by this evening; for they cannot have seen us, or winded us, and I expect they only had a suspicion that something was up; though they will be on the look-out for a time, they will be all right again by this evening."

Accordingly we withdrew a few hundred yards, to a sheltered place, and lay down, to spend the time till three in the afternoon, when the ibex would again be on the move.

There then occurred a rather lively altercation between Lassoo and Muksooda. The latter was very disappointed at what had occurred, and remarked that it would have been much better to have got a smaller one than none at all. This incensed Lassoo. He said that a man who did not try to get the very pick of a herd wasn't fit to be a shikari, and that Muksooda had better go and be a bear hunter if he had such low ideas. Lassoo, of course, had my support, and Muksooda retired, a bit down on his luck, for he knew quite well that he was in the wrong, and if he had been in Lassoo's shoes, would have done just what he had; and to be called a "bear hunter" is an awful thing! There is a certain class of shikari who go after bear only, and as artists they are held in much contempt, for a bear has only his ears and nose to depend on, his eyesight being very poor: he is but tame sport after ibex.

However, the moral atmosphere soon cleared, and Lassoo proceeded to make his pipe in the ground. This is a very simple arrangement. First, a stick is driven into the ground, making a hole about two inches deep, to act as the pipe's bowl. Then, from about a foot off, on the down hill side, another hole is made with a thin stick, connecting with the bottom of the first hole; this should be blown through to see that it is quite clear, it forms a tunnel, which is the stem of the pipe. A foot or so of a sort of dry hollow weed which grows about the place is stuck upright into the end of the tunnel; this is the mouthpiece, and behold! the pipe is complete. The big hole is the bowl, the tunnel the stem, and the hollow weed forms the mouthpiece. You lie down on your face to smoke it. The extraordinary thing about it is that it gives an uncommonly good and cool smoke. Lassoo enjoyed tobacco freely; but Muksooda was not allowed to smoke, as Lassoo said it was bad for his "wind," but all the same he used to have a suck at the pipe whenever he got a chance, and Lassoo wasn't looking. A great many hillmen do not smoke for this reason; and as a substitute they always carry snuff with them in a twist of paper; this they rub into their teeth, and they say it has very much the same soothing effect as a pipe. I tried it too, but gave it up as nothing like as good.

It was now about seven o'clock; and as we had lots of time to spare before three in the afternoon, my men found me a nice dry place out of the wind, and I got my book out, and had a read, then breakfast; and finally lit a pipe, and went over to where Lassoo and a party were smoking, some ten yards off, with their rugs over their heads, and their backs to the wind; for the day had clouded over, and a fine snow was falling, only to melt as it reached the ground. However, it was not bad as they had lit a fire; and we were soon talking and smoking quite merrily. Presently I noticed that the snow was beginning to lie a little, and not melt as it had been doing before. I made a casual remark to Lassoo to that effect, and he, on looking round, instantly ordered Chybra to get my things together, saying that we were going down the hill at once; telling me at the same time that we must be off as hard as we could go, or we should get stuck altogether, as, if the snow went on falling, the ground would get so slippery that we should not be able to move at all. We were soon in full swing down the ridge, going as fast as we could. The sky grew darker and darker, and the wind rose; and in no time we were white from head to foot, and could not see more than fifty yards before us. Gradually, as Lassoo had predicted, the ground grew more and more slippery as the snow deepened, until in half an hour we had to scratch it away before we put our feet down, as the grass shoes, now clogged with snow, no longer took a grip. These scratches got gradually deeper and deeper, until at last we were digging regular footholds, and proceeding at the rate of about two yards a minute.

Our course lay along a ridge which sloped downwards steeply enough; it was some five yards wide, and on either side fell precipitously into the valley below. Lassoo went first, I followed, and after me came Muksooda, and then Chybra. We were working our way along slowly, having to be very careful about each step, when suddenly something made me look towards Lassoo, who was some ten yards below me. What was my horror to see him flat on his

A FRESH FALL OF SNOW.

face, with his toes, knees, elbows, and stick all stuck hard into the ground; evidently having slipped. He lay like this a second, then my hair rose on end as he gradually began to slide, slowly at first, then quicker, his track, which lay along the ridge in the beginning, gradually curving towards the steep slope to the left, on, on he went, the pace getting faster and faster, until a cry broke from my men, "Lassoo 's gone!" He threw an agonized glance up towards me. Poor old Lassoo, he knew he had little or no hope; to hurry to his help was impossible, and he knew it. On he went, still doing all he could to check his speed, but in vain; five yards more and he would be over the edge, and then. . . . I shut my eyes to keep out the horrible sight that must follow; a second later, I opened them again, and found that he had stopped. What he had stopped against we could not see, because of the snow; but just as he had reached the very edge his foot had come up against a rock under the snow, and he was snatched from the very jaws of a horrible death. In a minute he was on his legs, and digging his way onto the ridge again, where we presently joined him; not, however, till Muksooda had also slipped, but had fortunately fallen against me, and stopped. "There is no use in trying to go on," said Lassoo, quite quietly. "We can't get down to the bottom; and if we have got to stay somewhere up here, there's no sense in going on till someone is killed. We will go for that rock, and wait till something happens." Accordingly we made for the rock he had selected, and under its shelter we sat. There was a clump of bushes close to it, and soon we had some sticks and a fire, and were fairly protected from the wind and snow; then I pulled out my pipe for a "soother."

"How much tobacco have you got?" said Lassoo.

"Oh, enough for a smoke all round. Where's your chillum?"

"You'd better keep as much as you can,"

said Lassoo; "you can't tell how long we shall be here."

"All right, I'll have some lunch then."

"What have you in the way of food?" said he.

"Two eggs and a bit of bread."

"Well, eat the bread if you are very hungry, but keep the eggs."

"Why, what do you anticipate, Lassoo?"

"I anticipate nothing," said he, "because God alone knows what He intends. But you see, sahib, we can't move till this snow stops and has melted again; no one knows when that will be; it may go on like this for several days."

This made me look round to see what sort of a time we were likely to have. The place we four were on was about four feet square, so that lying down would be out of the question. We had a very slender supply of sticks, very little food, and one blanket each; so it looked as if we were in for a bad time; however, it might clear up. It was now about nine a.m., and we sat and talked, and looked anxiously at the weather as we chattered with cold. Occasionally the wind dropped, and we began to hope that it would clear, but it always blew again with redoubled fury; presently the snow began to blow in behind our rock, and the fog got denser. Time crawled on; eleven came, but no change, except that the snow was getting visibly deeper, and now lay some four inches deep round us. Then we drew lots for choice of places for the night, not that there was much choice in the matter.

Presently quite suddenly the wind dropped, the clouds rolled away, and by noon the sun shone out warm, inspiring us with fresh courage and hope.

We held a council of war, which ended in our agreeing to work our way on, a hundred yards or so, to the end of our ridge, which ended in a precipitous drop right down to our village. It took us an hour to reach this point; a look through the telescope showed us the village at our feet, white in the snow, my bearer in the camp with a crowd of men round him, all scanning the hill, for they knew well enough that we must be stuck somewhere. A combined shout attracted their attention, and great was our joy to see a party with axes and hatchets start up the hill. We waited to see what route they would take, and then started slowly and carefully working our way down to them.

First, though, I ate my two eggs, and we finished the tobacco.

Three hours later and we rounded a corner to see these fine fellows cutting their way up to us; for it is one thing to go down hill, but quite another, and a much easier task to work one's way up when it's slippery. It's lovely to see a hillman climbing the mountain side; there is a fling about the whole thing that is indescribable; his rough, loose clothes offer no impediment to his movements, to the free, active swing of his brawny body and legs; at every point he is as different as possible from his brothers of the plains stagnating in their ease. He is a grand man, is the mountaineer, and he knows it; his active life and the many risks he braves leave a stamp on his character and his appearance which gives him an enviable nobility from which his poverty, his rough and almost squalid clothes do not detract.

Up the hill they came, those fine chaps, one behind the other, the first man making a mere scratch for his foothold, the next deepening it with his axe, until by the time the sixth man had made his cut there was a regular step. Now and then the leader (a post each took in turn) would slip, and be stopped with a laugh and a jest by the man next below him. At about five p.m. they were up with us, and much was their joy and ours as we all proceeded down together, reaching the bottom just as it was getting dark. I went to bed, but a sheep was killed for them in honour of Lassoo's escape and of their good day's work.

Next morning the skin of water which

had been put in my tent for warmth was found frozen solid, and I thanked my stars that the night had been spent in a warm tent with lots of bedding, outside a good dinner, and not 3,000 feet higher, in the open air, with only one rug, and an empty stomach!

CHAPTER V

A PROTRACTED CHASE

After breakfast we had the telescope out again, and after half an hour's search saw our ibex emerge from a small deep nullah low down the hill, where they had been driven by yesterday's snow; and, as we gazed, they came yet lower for their morning meal, proving conclusively that they had not been much frightened really, for in that case they would have been content to remain on the highest crags, and would have satisfied their appetites with the dry and tasteless grass of the peaks. We watched them carefully for a couple of hours as they grazed about, picking a scanty meal from among the newly fallen snow, which, however, was now melting fast under the influence of a generous sun, shining out of a perfectly clear sky.

THE "SCOUNDREL'S"

A very lovely morning it was, intensely cold, but with a hot sun. We lay watching the herd, each man taking the glasses in turn till his eyes grew tired, and then handing them on to someone else, while ever and anon an exclamation of joy would break from the gazer as our friend the ibex' horns would suddenly define themselves against a patch of snow, or a turn of his head would display them in profile; then anyone a grade higher than the onlooker would snatch the glasses from him, while he in a grade lower would humbly ask for a look, only to be refused, unless indeed the eyes of the possessor had grown particularly weary.

By this time the snow had melted in all the exposed places, and the mountains presented a singularly mottled appearance, the colouring of slope and dell, rock and glade, varying in exact proportion to its exposure to the sun's rays. On that ridge the grass was distinctly visible, and greener than yesterday, while the valley next it was quite white with newly fallen snow; here and there were partially melted patches, looking just as if the hillside had been powdered, while all over the place the wet rocks were glinting in the sunlight.

The herd was about two miles off, and not visible, even through the binoculars. In the search for it through the telescope landmarks were the only guide. "They are just by that big red cliff," Lassoo would say, or "near that shiny rock." The skilled use of the telescope is difficult of attainment, and it is a long time before one gets anything like handy with it. Imagine yourself looking through the glass; its field is very small, only a circle of some ten yards in diameter. All that is to be seen is perhaps an immense rock or a very clearly defined tree, which not being visible to the naked eye is not recognizable, and affords no clue: it is difficult to decide what the next step should be. The best way for a beginner is to have a look first with binoculars, and fix points in relation to the animals in the mind's eye; these, when he uses the telescope, give him a line to work on. But after a little practice some natural landmark, such as a well-defined valley, a lonely tree, or some such thing, is instinctively marked, and one puts the glass on to it as naturally as one puts food into one's mouth, or throws a gun up at a snipe. After a month or so of this, when the animals have once been found with binoculars, the mind seems to keep an involuntary register of the glass's wanderings, and the telescope strikes them at once.

Each member of the party ought to have his own telescope with him, and to practise looking through it constantly. Lassoo hardly ever had his eye off his; when he was doing nothing else he was always peering through it at distant objects, and that was why he was so much more proficient than any of us.

The ibex were rather late to-day, because of the snow and their yesterday's evening fast, and it was eleven before they settled down on their look-out post—very low to-day, as is usual after a new fall of snow, and in a most favourable place for us. Immediately above them was a small plain of snow, ending in a precipitous drop, a hundred yards beyond which cropped up the big rock on which they had taken up their position. We had, therefore, only to make a detour in order to get on to the plain, from whence we could approach within a hundred yards of them without a possibility of being seen; and right above them too! We were soon off; two o'clock saw us on the plain, and at 2.30 we were within a few yards of the point from which we expected to get a shot. A real chance this! Now absolute silence was the only precaution necessary, as the wind was favourable and we were out of sight. For the last fifty yards we executed a crawl to the edge; then Lassoo whispered, "Now I've done my part, let 's see you do yours. Sahib, look!"

I took off my puggree, and slowly got one eye over the edge; sure enough, there were the members of the herd sitting about on various shelves of the rock, while the two biggest were on its very top. One, a dark one, was lying with his side towards me, and the other, the light-coloured one, was a few yards nearer, on the extreme left edge of the rock, lying on his side, with his legs from the knee downwards stiff and sticking out over the edge, but his tail was towards me, the target a very small one. I threw an inquiring look towards Lassoo, who put his mouth to my ear and whispered, "Patience, sahib, he'll get up after a bit. Get your rifle on to him, and wait till he moves and gives you a certain shot."

I slowly worked my rifle over the edge and covered him, and then without moving the rifle withdrew my head, leaving one eye only over. A quarter of an hour passed and nothing happened. Then my ibex moved his head a little, and I thought he might be going to move, so I got my aim on to him; yes, I was sure he was going to rise. My finger gently pressed the trigger; a further slight movement of his body and my foresight covered . . . a rock! He had dropped over the edge without getting up. I changed my aim at once on to the other one, but he also was gone, and the next second they were all just visible bounding down the hill, and in a minute they were gone.

I was disappointed beyond words; but the thing was over, and no one apparently to blame. To this day *I* can't imagine how they spotted us. Even Lassoo said, "I'm afraid it is not written in his fate to die by our hand." There was nothing for it now but to go home as quietly as we could.

It seemed as if what Lassoo said was right, and that he was not for us, for the next day we again went up after him and were scented a mile off, and on the following day we were above the herd, and in a good position to begin the stalk, when a stray female, who had been away somewhere on her own account, suddenly appeared above and behind us and sent up the warning whistle. Then we went away for three days to another place, got a very good head, and came back for another try. We found them on a place we afterwards knew as the "fort," a buttress which commanded all the ground near them; at four o'clock they began to come down, as freely as possible, playing and gambolling, and taking a line which must have brought them quite close to us. Suddenly they all stopped and listened, while there came to our ears the distant report of a rifle, and the next moment they were off to their fort again, which was quite unapproachable, and which they declined to leave for two days.

On arrival at our camp we found that "the other sahib" had arrived at the foot of the nullah below us, and had shot a bear, five miles off; hence the noise which had cost us our ibex!

Every day we went up the hill again, in the hope that they might move; but move they wouldn't. The more difficult things became, the more we swore to have our friend! On the third morning the ibex did not return to the fort, but took up their post in another place. We made a tremendous detour and came to where they should have been. We had started from camp at five a.m., and got level with their grazing-ground at nine; we watched them go to their look-out post at ten, and then climbed hard till three. Our rage can be imagined when, on looking over the cliff, we found that they were not there, but back in their fort once more, about a mile off. I was sick with rage and disappointment. Luckily we had ordered our bedding to be brought half-way up the hill, so as to save us part of our climb; therefore we had not so very far to go back, and had no occasion to hurry home while it was light. Our herd soon afterwards left the "fort," and heading right away in quite a different direction, quitted this portion of the mountain, and went over into quite another valley two miles off. So we went to rest under a rock, arranged to have a final try next day, and decided that if we again failed we would leave the "scoundrel" for ever, as he was not an extraordinary head, and we were only persisting in hunting him out of pure "cussedness."

We reached the place we had chosen for the night as it was getting dark, and found the coolies just arriving with our blankets; so we set to work at once to collect dry grass for bedding, and wood for our fire, and soon had tea for all, and dinner, after which, and a smoke, we all went to our respective rocks. I had one, and the best one, to myself, while the others took what cover they could find.

There is nothing like the open air after all, when one has lots of bedding, and can keep warm. I always had an idea that lunacy was the fate of those who sleep in the moonlight, but that is evidently a delusion, for there generally was a moon of some sort, and five nights a week we slept with it full on us.

A really Arctic night it was, and my face

was stiff with cold while my body glowed with warmth. The luxury of abundance of bedding was a joy, and it was quite a pity to go to sleep, thus exchanging delight for unconsciousness! The sensation reminded me of my school-days, and I longed for my patient fag, who used to have to wake me every morning at four, so that I should enjoy the luxury of knowing that I had still got three hours of bed left, and that it was bitterly cold outside! Rather rough on the fag, you think? Yes, I suppose it was, but then I expect he soon got used to it, and awoke at four by habit; and besides, he had his fun in the day-time, when he could rely on my older arm for support, when his "side" roused the ire of his equals. And then, did he not always have the remains of my tea, and buttered toast, and suchlike benefits!

Alas! too short the night seemed, and daybreak saw us off again for the final effort. In three or four hours we reached the head of the valley into which the ibex had gone, and hard work it was, though we were going only very slightly upwards, for as the ground fell steeply away on our left, the grass shoes kept working round on our feet, which was very uncomfortable. We were very high up, too, and were constantly crossing snow valleys, where we had to cut footholds with the hatchet, as the snow was as hard as ice.

Crossing one of these, Lassoo slipped, and I involuntarily caught hold of him to help him, and the next second we were tobogganing down the snow. It is strange how small is the impression made by a danger which comes unexpectedly, and how great is one's confidence in luck and Providence. There were we, flying down the hill on our faces, with our sticks scratching over the hard snow, with death at no distant period apparently before us, and yet it never seriously entered my head that we should be killed. I only felt a peculiar coolness and a wonder as to what would stop us this time, while Lassoo's orders were quite distinct, "Work to the left as much as possible," which we proceeded to do by the help of our sticks, which acted as rudders. After about a hundred and fifty yards we managed to steer on to a big rock that cropped up through the snow, with no more harm done than a few scrapes and bruises. The whole episode was over so quickly that it was hard to grasp what a near thing it had been. I did not realize it till afterwards, when Lassoo expressed his displeasure that I should have presumed to think that I could more than look after myself.

Eight o'clock found us at the very head of the nullah into which the ibex had gone. We were full of hope that we should see them shortly, which hope was not belied; for Lassoo had not been away five minutes when he came back to say that they were coming up the valley towards us, and that we would have a shot at about two hundred and fifty yards. We then crept on over the ridge, and presently were looking down into the ibex' nullah. We were on the very edge of a precipice, a sheer drop of about three hundred feet; then came a ledge of rock, and beyond that we saw nothing but a vast empty space. The other side of the valley, consisting of rocks and snow, was steep too, but not quite so much so. Up the face of this we saw the herd of ibex slowly winding, picking the scanty grass as they came. Now one of them would rear up, as with his knees against the wall he reached for a more dainty morsel; now another would apparently do a straight-arm-balance, as with his forefeet on a lower ledge of rock he would take his precarious meal in perfect confidence. Then a larky young male would take possession of a post of vantage, blocking the path, and would threaten to contest the point, rearing and rearing as straight as a line, shaking his head the while and looking very fierce, only to give way on the leisurely approach of the head of the herd, who brooked no such games if they in any way affected him. The clash of horns was often heard in the quiet air, as two young bucks had a friendly battle on a ledge so narrow that it was inconceivable how any living creature could be there at all. Nearer and nearer they came as they rose higher up the mountain, until the leading female was nearly level with us, and the black chasm below alone separated us from our prey. A few yards more, and as she rounded a rock she stopped and had a look. No anxiety crept into her manner, and after a second she went on; then another came, and standing in exactly the same place had her look and went on; the third did the same; our coveted "big one" was sixth, and would doubtless do likewise, as this is their custom. Lassoo got his glass on to the place, and I drew a bead on the next one, so as to be ready to fire the moment my quarry appeared. The fourth came, stood a second, and went on. I was bitterly keen on getting the "scoundrel," so without thinking I rested my rifle on a niche in the rock, and with my left hand held the butt steady to my shoulder. Up came No. 5, and was gone. "Next one, sahib," said Lassoo. In a couple of seconds up strolled my friend, the bead was true on him, the trigger steadily pressed . . . bang! "Just over his back!" came from Lassoo with a muttered curse, while the whole herd went flying down the hill with huge bounds; the snow spurting up through their cloven hoofs as they pitched into it, sometimes dropping twenty feet at a time I should think. In a moment they were out of sight and gone.

We were all too mortified to say much, and few words passed between us. "Something wrong about the range that time," I said, "as I was quite steady." Now this was putting the blame on to Lassoo, who was responsible for the distance, and it "drew" him. He answered, "I could have killed him with my old Cashmeri rifle, and if yours isn't good enough for a shot like that, I'd sling it down the khud if

I were you and go back to Srinagar." "All right," said I. "You can throw further than I, see if you can throw it as far as that ledge, and then go back to Srinagar yourself and say you've lost your temper. Your friends will say you are a great shikari." And with that I swung off in a rage, and lay down in the shade of a rock to smoke and recover my temper, while Lassoo and party went off on a similar errand in the opposite direction. One pipe had no effect to-day, and no more had the second. So I had breakfast and two or three more pipes; then a snooze of a couple of hours; but still I was sulky and sick at heart, the inevitable result of a real burst of temper and of the blow to my pride, for I really fancied myself a good deal as a rifle shot, and there was no excuse I could think of for missing that time.

I lived the whole thing through over and over again. There they were coming up the hill, playing and gambolling; the first, second and third passed me; then the fourth came, and I drew a bead on him, but was not as steady as I could have wished; then I rested the rifle in the V in the rock; a flash went through my brain. I saw it all now. Fool that I'd been; of course my bullet had gone over the beast. I had broken a fundamental rule, had rested the rifle on a hard substance, and of course the muzzle had jumped up a little on the explosion of the cartridge. If it be necessary to rest the rifle at all it must be on something soft; either your hand or your puggree, or some substance that will "give." That's the last time I shall ever make that mistake; but it was an expensive experience, though I believe that no one ever learns without having to pay for it in coin of this sort. Here was the work of three weeks lost through a single mistake!

The next second I was with Lassoo, exclaiming, "I know how it happened." Poor old Lassoo was as sorry about the row we had had as I was, and he looked up much relieved, saying, "What was it, sahib?" I explained, and he said, "I knew it wasn't your fault, sahib, because you don't miss; but the distance was right I'm sure."

"Oh, yes, it was only my temper," said I, shaking his hand. "All red-haired sahibs are like that, but it doesn't last. I'm very sorry, Lassoo."

"No, no, don't say that," said he; "we all know you by this time, and you can say or do anything you like; we are your slaves, and you are the kindest master I have ever had; and I was angry too, and did not speak as I should have done. Forgive *me*, sahib."

"All right, have some baccy," and we were soon as happy as ever.

We stayed there till about three in the afternoon, and then went homewards, keeping an eye on the green slopes, for we thought we might get a red bear, and as I was leaving this place next day, and no longer minded disturbing it, I meant to shoot at a bear if I saw one.

When we had got about half way down the hill, we sat on a rocky point, overlooking a deep valley, bordered by a strip of verdant grass surmounted by a copse; there we lit our pipes, and waited in the hopes of seeing a bear come out to feed in the evening, as their custom is. We had been there nearly half an hour, and I was looking through the binoculars, when suddenly a red bear came tumbling out of the copse opposite to us in a great hurry, and bustled along down the green slope, going all sideways as he played down the hill, kicking out his hind legs, first on one side and then on the other, enjoying the perfect security of his lonely home among the mountains and trees. A glance at the lie of the ground between us, and our line was evident; we had only to get quickly down a ridge which ran rather to the left, then to change on to another on its right, under cover of a clump of trees, and then to run down that ridge, which ended up with a precipitous drop of perhaps three hundred feet into the valley below; the green slope on which the bear was feeding would then be directly opposite to us.

It was simple work after the careful stalking necessary for ibex, for poor old "harput" is very shortsighted, and as long as one does not cross a snow nullah within a quarter of a mile of him, no attention need be paid to his eyes. It is necessary, however, to be careful that the wind is not blowing towards him, for he has very good scent, and cracking sticks or other noises are perdition during the last bit of the stalk. In half an hour's free going we had got down to his level, and fifteen minutes of more careful stalking brought us to the extreme edge of the ridge, from whence he was clearly visible, two hundred yards away. The rock we were on fell sheer into the valley, which was perhaps thirty feet wide, being only the bed of a mountain torrent, which now looked like a snow road. From this the hill on the opposite side rose fairly steeply, having a patch of green grass just opposite us, rocky ground on our left, and a strip of birch forest running down to the valley on our right. In the grass opposite, and only a few yards away from the wood, stood a lonely oak, round which a small thicket of brambles and a few saplings had sprung up. When we reached the rocky end of our ridge we found ourselves in a most convenient place, for, hidden by the rocks, we could get a clear view of Bruin, and remain ourselves unseen. He was quite unconscious of danger, so that we had only to wait till he presented the best possible target, and then bag him. Just now he was right opposite to us, and on our level, feeding with his head down hill. He wandered about peacefully grazing, like a cow, sitting down on his haunches at times, and turning about in the peculiar way bears do. While we waited for a clear chance at him he got up and walked straight towards the solitary oak tree, behind which he disappeared. We looked for him to come out on the other side, but after five minutes Lassoo whispered: "Our luck has gone to Ladak; that bear has got a suspicion that something is up, and he won't come out of that till dark." "Well, then, drop a stone or something to frighten him, while I keep ready to fire," said I. Muksooda dropped a small stone over the edge of the cliff, and we heard it clattering over the rocks, but no signs of the bear; then he tried a larger one—no result; and finally, after five minutes, we were whistling as loud as we could, and hurling rocks down into the valley. Now, there being no question that we had been discovered, we proceeded to extremes. Lassoo crept a few feet down the cliff, and then fired into the bush; not a move. Then he took a careful aim at the oak tree itself; bang went the rifle; thud came the answer, showing that the bullet had hit the tree; and the next second old harput was bustling along, making for the strip of birch jungle. I waited my chance as he was going at full speed, and then, as they always do, he stopped to have a look round; my chance had come, and found me ready; the foresight was on him, the trigger pressed, and instead of the bang which should have laid him low, there came the sickening "click" of a miss-fire, while Bruin continued his course. Fifty yards more and he would be round the corner and out of sight, and as it was a branch of a tree was in my way, so that I had to stand up in order to fire; I arose with a muttered "no luck at all" on my lips, while I threw the rifle up like a gun, and pulled the trigger just on the off chance of hitting him. Great was my pleasure to see him roll over and over, head over heels, like a hedgehog, down the slope; and never stop until he lay dead on the clear white snow of the nullah below, and Lassoo with his skull cap off, bowing to me and saying in English, "Good morning"—by which he meant "well done."

It was growing late, so we started to get down to the bear's body, selecting the bed of a streamlet which fell down the cliff as our best route. It was but a deep cleft in the rock, and we proceeded down it with our hands on the wall on either side and our feet in the scanty but icy water. We got on quite well till within thirty feet of the bottom, when suddenly we found that the stream fell clear over the edge in a waterfall. Now what were we to do? We could not go back, as it would be a two hours' climb up to the top of the ridge, and it was getting dark; we had no food and this would be a very uncomfortable place to sleep in. Matters looked rather gloomy till after a search of some ten minutes we found a tree a little way up, the branches of which reached across to the next ridge. After a bit of a scramble we climbed over, and from there the way was easy. The bear proved to be five feet six inches long. Only a fair size, but with a most lovely coat, streaked with white in sympathy with the snow among which he had been living. By the time we had skinned him it was dark, but a fine moon served to light us home, which we did not reach till about midnight, as we were obliged to travel down the nullah until it struck the main one, up which we had to go to reach home, the cross-country route being impossible by the available light.

A skinned bear is very like a man, and his carcase is exactly like that of a human being who has had his head, hands and feet struck off; the impression it produced was unpleasant, and I was glad to leave it.

CHAPTER VI

FAIRLY IN THE WILDS

WE spent the next day in making arrangements for going into the wilds proper, as after we had left Metwan (where we now were), we should not see another village, and all our supplies would have to be brought from a distance.

Up to date we had had with us seven men from Lassoo's village who acted as coolies or carriers during the march, and made themselves generally useful when we were not on the move. Two of them were as a rule absent, on the road to and from Srinagar (which was one hundred and eighty miles away), getting letters and books, and taking letters, horns and skins. A third helped my "bearer" in camp to collect wood, water, eggs, milk, etc. for daily consumption, and in looking after our goats and sheep. A fourth was always up the hill with us carrying the lunch, and another was busily engaged in collecting supplies for me from the neighbouring villages and huts, while two more were constantly on the road bringing the main supplies of flour and wood for the shikaris and servants. Now, however, we were going right away from any civilization, indeed our furthest point would be about a hundred miles from Metwan, and as all supplies except those that could walk, such as sheep, would have to be carried out to us, more coolies would be required, and unfortunately the more coolies there are the more mouths there are to feed. Luckily it is customary that these extra "local" coolies get only their pay, and have to make their own arrangements for food; this is very little hardship to them, for they have lots of little brothers or relations, of about fourteen years old, who are just as well employed in taking their food out to them as in sitting doing nothing at home. The necessary number of extra coolies was therefore fixed by the number required to move our camp and the supplies for our original party, as, of course, in a place where no men live coolies cannot be procured just when they happen to be wanted, and our seven permanent coolies were already sufficiently occupied. Eventually we left Metwan with eight extra hands. Our meat marched with us in the shape of a small flock of hill sheep, as did also our milk, which was provided by four goats; while our fowls sat on the top of the loads and supplied us with eggs. The proportion of four goats to one man may seem excessive, but as they had to pick what food they could from among the snow they were very thin, and only produced a pint and a half of milk between them; besides, cold is almost as detrimental to the production of milk as starvation.

It was a funny start the next day. First went Lassoo, Muksooda, myself and the lunch coolie, to prepare the road for the load coolies in places where the hill track

A SNOW BRIDGE.

was broken away, or under snow; then came half a dozen coolies carrying their loads; after them my bearer driving along twelve sheep and four goats, and then the remaining coolies. Every variety of load they had too; most of them carried "kiltas," or leather-covered barrel-shaped baskets, carefully packed; another would carry the canvas of my tent; another, perhaps a bundle of tent poles. The fowls perched on the top of the loads if they were lucky, and managed to keep their balance, if not they were hung from them by the legs. This latter method I considered an atrocity and it was never adopted when I was looking on, though it was probably resorted to when I was not!

We started rather late the first day, and made only one short march, to get things into working order; we did not even trouble to undo the tents, but just slept under a rock.

Next day we made two marches, crossing the Zaig river by a snow bridge. It could hardly be called a bridge, as it was only about fifty yards long and a full two hundred yards wide. The snow over it was some ten feet deep, and had slipped as an avalanche from the hillside, and the river had forced a passage under it. It had fallen in in places, and was of course constantly melting, and subsiding into the torrent; it had deep fissures in it at the end we were approaching; the middle, having sunk, was perhaps five feet lower than the sides. Further on the snow was comparatively level, considering that it had fallen, not from heaven, but down from the mountain. A coolie crossed it, under my nose, at the near end, so I disregarded Lassoo's orders not to cross there, but higher up, and was punished, as usual, by getting a severe shock; for just as I was well in the middle, the snow suddenly gave an ominous crack right under my feet. Nothing more, it is true, but quite enough to be very alarming, for the idea of being launched, with a few tons of hard snow as playmates, into a tearing mountain torrent is not a pleasant one,

OUR CAMP. EVENING.

especially as the prospect of ever getting out is nil.

We bivouacked again that night; and as we had seen nothing good enough to shoot there, went on next day to the foot of a branch nullah, in which Lassoo said we should see some good "heads."

There we pitched our camp, and taking four men with us, with bedding and food for three days, as well as two goats, we set off up the branch valley. A steep, narrow little valley it was; quite precipitous and inaccessible on the left, though fairly easy on the right-hand side. We had not gone a couple of miles when we saw a herd of ibex, only four in number, but all good ones. They were up in the crags on the left, and as our route up the valley itself, the only possible one, was commanded by them, we were unable to move till dusk, when we went on to a clump of rocks, and there stopped for the night. At two a.m. we started up the valley, which looked like a snow road, and arrived by five a.m. as near to the ibex as we dared. Shortly afterwards the day began to break, while we shivered with cold behind our rock. At six a.m. we spotted the herd in nearly the same place as yesterday, and by ten the ibex had gone to their look-out post; still we could not move. We then had breakfast, a smoke and a read; then sleep, tea, and read again till it was eight o'clock. Then the herd began to graze, but still we could not move without being seen, so we waited till dusk, and then went back to our bedding again. The next day was a repetition of its predecessor, and we determined that the day after we would try to reach a point a couple of miles further on, and endeavour to get up the hill from there. Accordingly, we started shortly after midnight, and went stumbling along in the dark over the snow, always up the snow covered river, and arrived at the desired point while it was still dark. Then our bedding was sent on a mile further to a place where a fire could be lit without danger of disturbing the game. We found the ibex again at dawn, but could get no nearer as the cliff proved inaccessible.

In the evening they moved higher up the nullah. We hoped now to get a chance, as they had got into more possible ground; but next morning they were nowhere to be seen. So leaving the camp where it was, we worked slowly up the nullah to see if they had gone that way. We had not seen them by eleven, and so the lunch coolie was sent back to bring the bedding up to where we were. No signs of them in the evening, and there was nothing for it but to go on next day.

Just before dinner I went over to Lassoo's fire, and saw them all just about to have dinner. To my surprise they had only chupatties (unleavened cakes) and boiled wild rhubarb. "Not much of a meal tonight, Lassoo," said I.

"No, sahib."

"And why so abstemious?" I asked.

"Well," Lassoo answered, "the truth of

the matter is, that I don't know whether the ibex have gone up the nullah or down, and I consequently can't send any coolies back to camp for food, for fear they might disturb them, if they're that way; and we only brought food for three days."

Now we had been away four days, and might be away four more, so that without a murmur these poor chaps were starving themselves of their own free will. My bearer, I found, had plenty of food, so I gave them all I did not want. They are the right sort, these hillmen!

Next morning we pushed on a bit further, leaving the bedding where it was, and soon found our friends. I was overjoyed, but Lassoo was silent. After watching them for a quarter of an hour, he said, "Now I understand what they've been doing; there is a snow leopard after them." "How do you know?" I asked. Lassoo handed me the glasses, and I looked. The ibex were among the crags and snow, but instead of grazing about, as is their wont, they were all four standing on separate rocks, gazing downwards. Presently one made a dash and a bound on to another rock. Such a bound! Why even with the glasses at two miles, it looked tremendous. Then another dropped from his ledge, and was presently silhouetted on another crag. This sort of thing continued the whole day. No rest in the middle of the day. There they stood, and looked, and looked, straining to detect their unseen enemy. "How does a leopard ever get them?" I asked. "Just stalks them fair and square, and then seizes them: if he can't get them in one day, he goes on till he can. I've seen young ones that have been killed by a leopard, but never an old male. I don't think they often get him."

Towards evening the poor ibex evidently had had enough of this, or else they had located their enemy, for they suddenly left their post, and came as hard as they could pelt right away to the precipitous and inaccessible cliff that towered immediately above us.

Early next morning we set off, got on to the top of this cliff by a long detour, and by three were looking over the edge; and, sure enough, there they were, right below us, all four of them; but the cliff was so jagged and steep that we could only get glimpses of them at intervals. Back we went to our bedding, returning again early next day, but with the same luck. We saw them all right, but couldn't get a shot at them! The third day we searched for them in vain; quite suddenly, however, at about eleven, Lassoo spotted them on the very top of the hill, sitting on a ledge only a few feet from the edge of the cliff. "Now 's our chance, sahib," said Lassoo, "if you're on for a fast thing. They will be there for three hours; and we must get there before they move, or we shall have the same thing happen again." I answered by pulling up my belt a hole and starting. What a pace we went, up and up, each man going quite independently and resting when he wanted to. I was fit now, and it was "my day out," and that day I was as good as any of them, so that by two we were on the sloping plain of snow which topped the cliff where our ibex had been. The lunch coolie was then made to sit behind a rock, and we three went on. Now we were within a hundred yards of the edge, and we crawled along without a sound, hardly daring to breathe, for we knew the animals should be within a few yards of us. Then Lassoo looked carefully over, but saw nothing. Perhaps we had not located the spot properly. Then he crawled a yard or so to the right, and then tried a bit to the left. Suddenly he drew back and beckoned me to look. I did so, and my heart stood still as I saw, not ten yards off, the head and horns of a fine ibex directly below us, gazing down into the valley beneath. I withdrew my head, not knowing what to do. It was not much of a target, so I waited, and then crawled a yard to the right, to see if I could in any way get a better sight of him. Again I peered cautiously over, and what was my surprise to see a second exposed to view, lying close to him, at full length on his side and yawning; and he was the better of the two. Lassoo also had a look, and nodded to me to shoot. It 's one thing to look with one eye over the edge of a cliff at an ibex ten yards off, and quite another to get a shot at him, for in the latter case your rifle, head, and shoulders have to be got over before firing is possible, and quickness of sight is the ibex's keenest faculty. I never had such a strain on my nerves before; it seemed to be an hour before I had got the bead on to him, and it was, I should think, quite three minutes. First, the rifle muzzle had to be poked over the edge, and then ever so gradually pushed out and out till the weapon was at the balance; then, just as slowly, head and shoulders had to be got out; Muksooda holding my feet the while to prevent me from falling over the cliff.

Imagine yourself in the position. After a considerable amount of danger, privations and work in the pursuit of this individual animal, two long and tedious days of fruitless climbing; two long, weary night scrambles up the snow valley; several cold nights with somewhat scanty bedding; a very hard bed; not too much to eat; and a few rather "near things" on the hill; and here you are within a few feet of your prize. Imagine how anxiously you would keep your eye on him, as he lies indolently on his side just beneath, with one of his sleepy, half-shut eyes directly facing you, and you know that any movement that may attract his attention will make him open those eyes, and that he will then be gone and no chance of firing; while at any moment he may wake up in the ordinary course of events. Surely you can feel the insane desire to get the thing settled one way or the other—it does not matter which way—and yet you have got to pull yourself together and do the right thing;

which undoubtedly is, to move as slowly as possible. Now the bead covers him, and it is hard even now to refrain from fluking the whole thing and pulling the trigger! However, as a matter of fact, one presses the trigger slowly, carefully. No resting the rifle on a rock this time; head cool, hand steady, a steady and increasing strain on the trigger, and . . . bang!

. The next thing visible was the ibex bounding down the hill. I let fly another shot, splash went the bullet within an inch of him. Then another fine chap passed me like a flash, and I had a try at him, but the bullet struck a little low; then a glimpse of yet another as he stood startled on a crag a hundred yards off. A steady aim this time, and just as I pressed the trigger he was gone, and though the bullet sped, I knew it was too late. "Never mind, sahib," said Lassoo, "you have got one." "No," I said, "I'm afraid I have not, as I saw every bullet as it hit, but I can't understand missing that first one." Lassoo pointed down the cliff, and there, sure enough, was my first ibex, in the last throes of death, with his hind feet dug in the ground, kneeling up against the hill, with his forehead on the snow. As I looked, a shiver passed over him, his hind legs bent more and more, and the next second he had rolled over slowly, then, gathering way, his pace got faster and faster, his body lurched and bounded down the hill, and at last he pitched clear over a ledge, shooting out into space, all legs and horns, an object which made my hair stand on end, and formed the subject of nightmares for months afterwards. "What infernal luck," hissed Lassoo, "his horns will be smashed to bits." We then left everything, and crawled carefully down to where our game had vanished from sight, hoping to locate his carcase, as Lassoo said that he had probably fallen down nearly to our camp. At first we could see no signs of him, but suddenly discovered his body about a hundred feet off, jammed between two rocks, which had, mercifully for us, caught him and saved his horns. Yes, there he was, sure enough, with his head hanging backwards over space, his forelegs doubled up on his chest, his hind ones dangling, and his white stomach turned up to the sky. How to get him was the question. His position seemed to me inaccessible. When, however, Muksooda and the coolie took off their shoes and coats and crawled down the face of the cliff, I saw, for the first time in my life, what a hillman can do if he is put to it. Lassoo, in the meantime, escorted me by another route to within thirty feet of my prize. When I arrived, Muksooda and the coolie were nearly down to the body. I would not have gone with them for all the gold of the Indies, and what is more, I do not believe any man could have gone down that wall who had not feet with about as much feeling as the sole of a boot, and a big toe capable of bearing his whole weight for minutes at a time. It was quite creepy enough work seeing them even. However, they arrived without mishap, and instantly measured the horns with their hands. "Very thick horns, but only thirty-five inches," shouted Muksooda; "and not a breath in him, so he can't be 'hilaled.'" "What a pity," said Lassoo; "for a good meal of meat would have done us all good." The process called "hilal" is that of cutting an animal's throat, repeating the prayer laid down by Mahomed for the occasion. No true follower of the prophet would think of eating the meat of an animal which had not been thus treated, any more than he would eat the flesh of the unclean and forbidden pig. They are very strict about this, only very low caste men ever fail, and many a good meal have I seen wasted in this way. They do not, however, require that much life should be in the animal, and if he has a breath anywhere in him, that is quite good enough for their scruples.

On one occasion I was standing by a barasingha, which I had killed, and we could not find a breath anywhere in him, so had given up all thought of "hilal." Suddenly, however, he moved a leg, through muscular contraction after death, whereupon the men cut his throat with great joy, murmuring the prayer laid down in the Koran. This ibex, however, was a hopeless case, so his head was cut off, he was skinned, and his carcase left for the vultures, while the trophies were pulled up by Lassoo and myself by a rope made out of our combined puggrees knotted together. We were joined by Muksooda and the coolie half an hour later, and were soon back on our cliff again on our way home.

What a jolly return that was! For instead of having always to keep something between us and the ibex as before, we made tracks boldly down a valley of snow, which was now nice and soft, and after a few hundred yards walking, each man spread his blanket under him, and went tobogganing down. How we did fizz along as we lay on our backs, trusting entirely to the valley for our direction! Away we went at lightning speed for perhaps ten minutes, and were landed almost at our camp, having converted our many hours of ascent into a few minutes of descent. It gives a pleasant, comfortable feeling does success; and we had a rather prolonged smoke that night, and Lassoo told us many tales about the various sahibs he had been with at one time or another. One of them I remember used to go up the hill with four men and a rope to pull him along, and always had a small camp table and chair taken up with him for meals.

"That was a bad one," said I.

"Oh, no, he wasn't," retorted Lassoo.

"But he must have been. How could you stalk ibex with a retinue of men like that?"

"Oh! as far as shooting was concerned of course he was bad, although he got a few all the same; but he was very kind to us when we were sick, and would have done anything to help us."

"Well, but any sahib would do that."

"No, sahib, they don't. Some of them think that we are made of wood, and expect us to do anything, while they do nothing, and seem to forget that we want food and clothes just as much as they do. We attach greater importance to a sahib being kind than to anything else. You see we are far away from our homes, and unless we are looked after and treated fairly we get sick; and you must remember that to a poor working man health is everything. If we get sick and can't work, what's to happen to our wives and children?"

"Now," he continued, "I'll tell you how you came to get the coolies to come over the Mergen Pass. Do you remember that old shikari who was so ill and poor, and to whom you gave five rupees? Well, when I had collected the coolies for the pass, at the last minute they got nervous, and said that it was all very well, but what would happen if any of them got hurt? 'Why,' said I, 'the sahib will look after you, and nurse you, and give you wages till you get well. He is not stingy, my sahib! Look how he was sorry for poor shikari Gafara, and gave him five rupees and a coat; and ask Hayard how he nursed him when he had fever, and gave him medicine and his own bedding.'" (I had as a matter of fact only given him a spare rug and some quinine.) "'Oh, you are all right, he will look after you!' That was the last objection anyone made; I got them over as you know. You've done the wisest thing in the world in being kind to us, because before a shikari goes with a sahib, he always finds out about him, and you'll have no trouble next time. You would be surprised what a lot we know about anyone who has been shooting."

"Do you know anything about 'Badger' in my regiment?" I asked. "He was in the Pir Punjal last year with Rahim."

"Of course I do. Wasn't he the sahib who walked forty miles into Srinagar with his second shikari, who got mauled by a bear, and gave up a week's shooting to look after him? Oh, yes, we know him well."

"Did you know anything about me, Lassoo?"

"Not much, but we got a good character of you, and heard that you had nursed a servant of yours who had cholera; and we thought you were the right sort when we heard of the way you scored off Akbar that time when he wouldn't produce coolies."

"So you heard that," said I laughing. "Well, you do know something, I must say."

"Tell us the story," said Chybra; which I did.

It was simple enough. I had been in the Pir Punjal the year before, and I had had a very bad shikari, whom I got for only three weeks. We had great luck, however, till at last we came to a place which Akbar said was a real good one. For five days we searched the land, but saw nothing; so I ordered a move for next day. Next morning there were no coolies, and I had to wait. Akbar promised them for the next day, but failed again. Then I found out by chance that Akbar's village was near, that all our supplies came from his house, where he went at night, and that that was the reason why he wanted to remain there. Next day there were again no coolies, so I sent for Akbar and told him that as this place was useless, if he did not get coolies, we should have to carry the things ourselves. In the morning there were again no coolies. So I ordered the loads to be made up. There were six in all, and with our three coolies, the two shikaris, and myself, we marched. Under ordinary circumstances a shikari is far above carrying a load, but when I did it myself, he could not well demur, and though I was absolutely dead at the end of the march, Akbar was just as much so; and I had the sense of a score to help me along, while he had not. I never had any more bother with coolies after that.

A laugh followed, and I asked Lassoo what he thought of sahibs generally. "As you know, sahib," he said, "we all believe in them, as you can see yourself, for you remember that 'case' they asked you to settle at Wardwan; well, I hear there has been no more talking about it, they have all submitted to your decision. But still there are some queer ones about. I know one who came to a mountain near here, and he spent six months after one moth, and was delighted when he'd got it. Just fancy climbing about for six months after one insect.[1] Can you imagine that?"

"Do you know, Lasso," I replied, "that there are many people in England who live in towns, with comfortable houses and fires, who would think I was a lunatic to come away alone here, and sleep in the snow, and have nothing to eat but mutton, eggs, and tea, all for an occasional chance at an ibex? You must remember that to that man, that particular butterfly was the same as a forty-incher to us."

[1] "Klira," a generic term which includes butterflies and worms!

"Yes," he replied, "I see that; a rare insect to him is the same as a forty-incher to us. But what a funny amusement, sahib!"

"Now tell me, Lassoo, did you ever see a sahib who really funked?"

Lassoo grew grave, and said, "I've been a shikari thirty years, and I only saw one case of it; and that was when I was with a Major P. When we were charged by a red bear he regularly ran away, and we should all have been killed, only I hit the bear on the nose with my stick, and she turned away. I told the sahib that I wouldn't go out with him again, and that I was going back to Srinagar; but he said that he was very, very sorry, that he couldn't account for it, and that a devil must have got into him. So I didn't go away after all; and the funny part is, that I had had all sorts of adventures with the sahib before, and had more after; and that was the only time anything of the sort occurred. I think a devil really must have got into him at the moment, for he ran nearly half a mile without stopping."

We then turned in under our various rocks. On this occasion I had a very comfortable one, small it is true, but hanging well over, almost to the ground, and long enough to provide perfect shelter, though I had to crawl to get under it, and could not sit up when there. I was soon fast asleep and pursuing ibex in my dreams; not on the ordinary methods, but on that of the snow leopard, as Lassoo had described it. Now I crawled, lay in wait, and crawled again; now I neared my prey, which was expecting me from below; now I prepared to spring, and bury my fangs in his throat; suddenly the ibex looked full at me, and instead of being petrified with terror, as he ought to have been, to my horror advanced steadily towards me, and was upon me with one wild bound. How his sharp toes dug into my back! I seized him by the neck and held him with ease, while he bleated gently and I awoke, hitting my head hard against the roof of my bedroom. Was I still dreaming? No! I could smell ibex; I was gripping wet wool. I ran my hands up to where his horns should be, and I found I had got hold of one of my goats. Poor beast! it was snowing hard outside, and she had come in wet and miserable for shelter; so I let her have a corner of my bedding, and we both slept the rest of the night undisturbed. It's a rum thing to sleep with a wet goat!

When I awoke it was fairly late, but quite fine again; the country looked lovely with its fresh coat of snow, and soon, having had breakfast, we made tracks for our tents, which we reached safely in the afternoon. Then I had a bath and a general clean up, and was hardly dressed again when a coolie arrived from Srinagar with letters and some new books. I speak somewhat lordlily about "dressing" and "cleaning up," but I mean no deception: my bath was a hole dug in the ground, with my waterproof sheet laid over it. All the clothes I owned were two knickerbocker suits and two flannel shirts (which latter served as night-shirts as well), plenty of socks, and six handkerchiefs. Sponge I had none, nor had I a basin, bedstead, or table; but I had soap, a low camp chair, a uniform box (which made an excellent table), and the nearest stream for my basin. I had also a toothbrush, writing materials, and books, and most useful of all, a fur-lined great-coat. I had by this time what I considered a fine beard, and when I had my puggree on, and my close-cut hair was no longer visible, I considered I looked very well. Lassoo thought so too, he said.

We had now time to look about us: the last week had done wonders. When we started up the small nullah a week ago it was winter, now it was spring; the snow had melted a great deal; the grass was a bright green everywhere; the birch forests no longer looked dead, but were bursting with tiny green shoots, and Lassoo predicted that our troubles were over, for now the ibex would be tempted down by the green grass, and we should have no more long climbs.

It was now June, and Lassoo said that in ordinary years it was like this in April. Certainly it was lovely, and with the exception of occasional snow-storms we had no bad weather at all afterwards. As the season was advancing, and as we were steadily rising up the valley, we moved with the spring, and had this class of weather the whole way. The next month work was very easy compared with what we had had, and we did very well as far as the amount of sport went; but I did not see a really fine head, though I got five fair ones; but the month after I did see one, and spent four weeks after him. He was right up at the very end of our valley, on a mountain known as "Nun Kun," in very bad rocky ground, and though I devoted a month to him, I never got a fair chance, though I did risk a long shot on the very last day, and missed.

Then we had to make back for Srinagar as quickly as we could, as we had only just time enough left to get back before my time was up. As we no longer had supplies to carry, our loads were light; and we were able to shove along at our best pace, and got to Metwan without adventures, doing two marches a day. The only difficulty we encountered was the crossing of the Zaig river. You will remember that we crossed it before by the snow bridge, which of course had long since melted away, and we were now obliged to construct a footbridge over it. It was a pretty roughly made thing, consisting of two pine trees which, felled one from either side of the river, lay side by side bridging the torrent, while for a footway roughly split logs were laid across them, the whole forming a path two feet wide. As the split pieces of wood were of all shapes and sizes, and not fastened down in any way, they moved a little underfoot, giving an unpleasant feeling of insecurity, the waters of the swollen river, moreover, tearing along underneath, caught the eye and produced giddiness, and there was of course nothing in the shape of a handrail to help. Crossing was not much of a difficulty to me or the shikaris, who had got used to most things by this time; nor to the coolies, who had been born and bred among the hills; but it completely floored my bearer, who had lived in security in the tents below, and I was really afraid we should never get him over at all. He could not make up his mind to have a try, but stood trembling on the brink, wringing his hands; so I went back, and told him to go over on all fours, but he simply dared not. Then a coolie offered to carry him over, but he struggled off his back at the last moment, and I began to think we were a fixture on the banks of the Zaig. However, finally our efforts were crowned by success; we blindfolded him and tied him on to a coolie's back! When he found that it was useless to struggle he gave in, and went over without moving a muscle, except those of his lips, which worked rapidly as he vowed to present numberless sheep to the poor in honour of God if he only got over safely.

It was hard to imagine that this was the same country we had come through two months ago, then all naked rocks, snow, and bare trees; now it was covered waist high with luxuriant grass and flowering weeds, and the then dry copses were dense green strips of forest. The river at Wardwan, which we had waded, was now a howling, roaring, foaming torrent, with a new bridge over it; and our former route down the Mergen Pass was now a hill river, surging down a steep mountain gorge, our new course running along the ridge of the mountain, knee deep in luscious grass. On our way along this path, we passed quite close to the spot where we had got our first ibex, ages ago it seemed. Four days more and we were in Srinagar; had had a

A VILLAGE ON RETURN JOURNEY.

photo taken of our "heads," had settled up all accounts, and there was nothing left but to take boat and get down forty miles to Bara Mullah, whence in two days stage tongas would take me to Rawal Pindi, the nearest railway station. Lassoo came down a bit of the way with me in the boat, and then said "Good-bye." I thanked him for all his kindness and forbearance, and was just miserable when I saw the last of him. Poor old Lassoo! he began to say something, but stopped suddenly, gripped my hand in both his, and then quitted abruptly. I saw his back shaking with sobs as he hurried away. Dear old Lassoo! he was a good man and true, and I number him among my very best friends. I spent the day with a lump in my throat.

Next morning found us at Bara Mullah, where I had breakfast in the staging bungalow with two other fellows who had been shooting for the first time. They had both given it up in a month because it bored them; one because he had got sick of eating mutton, and the other because he had only got five heads in a month, one of which was a thirty-eight incher! Some people are hard to please!

Two days later we passed through the hill station of Murree about lunch time. I had on my best pair of knickers and a clean grey flannel shirt. I had a beard, too, bushy and red, and, on the whole, rather fancied myself; but I gathered from what I heard that my appearance was not universally appreciated, for when we went into the hotel lunch-room, which was full of lovely ladies in gala clothes, for the Murree races were on, I saw one enslaver toss her head towards me as she said to her friend the single word "prehistoric." She blushed deeply as I betrayed my appreciation of the description.

THE END.